_f_**P**

D0169944

And the Heart Says Whatever

Emily Gould

Free Press

New York   London   Toronto   Sydney

Free Press
A Division of Simon & Schuster, Inc.
1230 Avenue of the Americas
New York, NY 10020

First Free Press trade paperback edition May 2010

FREE PRESS and colophon are trademarks of Simon & Schuster, Inc.

For information about special discounts for bulk purchases, please contact Simon & Schuster Special Sales at 1-866-506-1949 or business@simonandschuster.com.

The Simon & Schuster Speakers Bureau can bring authors to your live event. For more information or to book an event contact the Simon & Schuster Speakers Bureau at 1-866-248-3049 or visit our website at www.simonspeakers.com.

Designed by Carla Jayne Jones

Manufactured in the United States of America

1   3   5   7   9   10   8   6   4   2

Library of Congress Cataloging-in-Publication Data

Gould, Emily
And the heart says whatever / Emily Gould.
p. cm.
1. Gould, Emily. 2. Authors, American—21 century—Biography. 3. Editors—United States—Biography. I. Title.
PS3607.O8845Z46 2010
818'.609—dc22
[B]   2009042229

ISBN 978-1-4391-2389-8
ISBN 978-1-4391-3734-5 (ebook)

Names and identifying characteristics have been changed and certain situations and characteristics are composites.

To I.D. and W.D., D.G. and the memory of A.G.

Contents

And the Heart Says Whatever

Introduction

One of my tasks at my first job had been to stand at the locked doors near the elevator bank and lead guests inside. I would stand in the doorway and wait and, when I heard the ping of the elevator reaching the publishing house's floor, I'd start smiling. After shaking the guests' hands I would lead them into the little waiting area where there were two armchairs and a little table next to a rack of our newest shiny hardcovers, and I'd bring them coffee or tea or water and then go sit back down at my desk. Then, when my boss was ready—he let some people wait longer than others—he'd tell me to go and get them, and I'd lead them through the maze of the office, chatting brightly over my shoulder. If the person or people walking behind me were men, I would be conscious of their eyes following the movement of my back, conscious always that I was like the books displayed in the waiting area: an ornament that demonstrated the company's power. The ritualistic aspect of this duty appealed to me the same way waiting tables had. Sometimes the guests would ask to use the restroom on the way to my boss's office and I would wait for them outside it until they finished peeing.

No one was waiting at the door to greet me when I showed up at the Gawker office for my job interview. If I hadn't gone to a party there a few months earlier, I would not have immediately known it was an office at all. Later, after I started working there, I learned that people would wander in off the street all the time, mistaking it for an Internet café. The space would have made a good café— it was in SoHo, and there were plenty of laptops—but as things were, there wasn't even a coffee machine.

I told one of the laptop people the names of the men I was there to see and sat down on the couch in the front of the office to wait. It was around lunchtime, and the smell of trapped gases given off by warm food in takeout containers filled the room. There was a low coffee table in front of the high-backed couch with piles of tabloid weeklies arrayed on it: *Us, Star, In Touch*. But they were back issues, much older than ones you'd find in any doctor's office. I flipped through one of them, looking up periodically to see if my interviewers were headed over, and during one of these glances my eye caught on a scarf hanging on a coatrack near the door. The scarf was black and gold, from H&M—it was the scarf I'd lost on the night of the party! I went over to the rack and was in the act of draping it around my neck when they finally came over to greet me.

In another half hour or so I was walking out, wearing the scarf, wondering how things had gone. They hadn't asked a lot of questions; they'd mostly told me what the job would entail and asked if I thought I could handle it, and I'd said "sure." Throughout the interview I'd wondered whether the laptop people, eating their take-out lunches from containers next to their keyboards at the long black tables just a few feet behind us, were listening to our conversation. I'd made one joke that had gone over well: gesturing to the old tabloid magazines, I'd bragged that in addition to my publishing expertise, I was such an aficionado of celebrity gossip that I could list the last five people Jennifer Love Hewitt had dated. Luckily no one had asked me to name them.

I got the job. I started bringing my laptop to the office and setting it down at the long black table among the other laptop people. Some were programmers who kept their heads turned towards their monitors for hours at a time as they immersed themselves in code. But the others were bloggers like me.

My job was to write twelve posts a day about "media gossip," which meant anything unpleasant or otherwise intriguing about anyone who had power in any Manhattan culture industry. There had to be enough posts so that whoever was sitting at my old desk at the publishing house, and everyone in Manhattan like her, could read something new whenever boredom struck, as I'd done. The posts could be as short as a few sentences explaining a funny photo or as long as a little article, a "field guide" about some person I was puncturing or promoting, or promoting by puncturing. Some posts were gleaned from the e-mails the site got from anonymous tipsters, who would forward us memos from their bosses, repeat rumors about their coworkers and higher-ups, and ask us to investigate news stories they found suspiciously lacking in salacious detail. I would investigate by quoting their anonymous allegations on the site and asking if anyone else knew anything more. The rule for tips was that if three people wrote in about the same thing, we probably ought to do a post about it, no matter how dumb it seemed. My coworkers and I would claim the tips we were interested in following up on by forwarding the e-mail back to the tips address with the word TAKING appended. Sometimes, especially if a tip seemed like it would be easy to make into a post just by tacking on a little context, a joke, and the word *allegedly*, more than one of us would TAKE it simultaneously and then we would have to figure out who was better suited to writing up the item, or who'd replied first, and the race to claim the good tips meant that our attention was continuously divided between the post we were currently writing and the constant hunt for the post we'd write next. Another attention-suck was the useless but irresistible impulse to skim the dozens or even hundreds of comments on my previous posts. Most of them were poisonous to some degree, and many of them seemed like they might be from young assistant types who knew more than I did, because they were still working at these companies.

People came in for meetings on the couch where my meeting had been and I didn't hear a word they said. I put a coffee cup down on my desk and a month later I noticed that it was still there, the sludgy centimeter of once-liquid inside it long since congealed into a cloudy gray pudding.

My rule for myself was that if I could get two posts into the queue by nine I could afford to spend the ten minutes it would take for me to wait in line for a coffee and a tartine from Balthazar Bakery. This line would devolve into a scrum of loud, disorganized shoppers by lunchtime, but the early morning crowd was manageable, chic, and friendly, people who worked in Soho's boutiques and boutique ad agencies. The conversations I overheard them having told me something, I thought, about what the people sitting at their desks reading my posts were thinking about. Sometimes I fantasized that they recognized me, and as my photograph began to appear on the site more often, eventually some of them did.

I admired the Balthazar employees, the way they danced around each other with studied grace as they fulfilled their patrons' picky requests. They were under constant pressure to turn out standardized soy lattes in strictly delimited time windows, and they did it without seeming panicked or frustrated. I, on the other hand, would spend every minute in line besides the ten I'd carved out for the errand in a frenzy of tortured antsiness, with a reel of potential post topics unspooling continuously behind my eyes.

The moment I filled the day's quota, I slammed my laptop closed and went home to Brooklyn. Sometimes when I got there I had to turn around immediately to cover a party back in Manhattan.

It wasn't the first or the last of these nights that I remember most vividly; instead I remember one somewhere in the middle, when I was starting to get used to what I was doing. That night, I changed quickly into a borrowed black dress that, even though it was from Zara, seemed like it might pass for something a rich person would wear. I was going to a book party for a *Devil Wears Prada*–style roman à clef about working for one of the most legendarily terrifying bosses in book publishing, which was being held at the Soho loft of rich friends of the author's.

The subtitle of all our party report posts would be "Team Party Crash," even though it was often the case—it was that night—that I had not just been invited but solicitously goaded by a publicist into attending.

I emerged from the subway a few minutes sooner than I'd intended. I walked once around the party block, then twice, being careful not to arrive too early.

The elevator opened into the apartment itself; I had expected a hallway, but instead there was a uniformed attendant, smiling impersonally and offering to take my coat. I wondered whether I had a dollar bill with which to tip her later to get it back, and whether that was even something you did in someone's apartment. Behind the attendant the room was brightly lit, huge, and full of people. A woman's burnished back gleamed in a backless nude jumpsuit. Another woman's dress had a feather appliqué. None of these outfits, it seemed safe to say, came from Zara. The richly tanned leather furniture and the made-up skin and the leather couches that my studiously casual glances skimmed all seemed to have the same sumptuous texture. Whether this had something to do with lighting or the surfaces themselves was impossible to determine.

The solicitous publicist who'd invited me made a beeline for me and, in a hushed tone, pointed out the important people in case I'd missed them. I heard a mixture of fear and forced jollity in her voice, and I thought about how a few months ago at the publishing house where I'd worked I had knocked deferentially at the door of her counterpart there before entering and, in the politest way possible, asked her to do something on behalf of one of my boss's authors.

I excused myself and found the bar.

After a drink everything began to seem less terrifying and more exciting, and I let myself stop thinking, for a moment, about how I'd describe it. I saw another gossip writer and felt a familiar surge of relief and gratitude; I could talk to him while I finished this first drink, and warm up to the conversations I'd need to have with people I would try to prod into saying something ridiculous enough to reiterate in tomorrow's post.

A pretty, intense woman who had married the heir to something banal but lucrative spent some time telling me about what breast-feeding was like, clearly angling to have her swollen cleavage photographed by the Gawker photographer who alternately trailed me and wandered off when I spent too long chatting with someone he deemed unimportant or uninteresting-looking. The uniformed attendants circulated with hors d'oeuvres. A man who wore a blazer over a screen-printed T-shirt—he'd changed out of his work clothes into his casual outfit— told me that I looked like I "belonged in the East Village." This was a year after Neil Strauss's book about being a pickup artist had been published but a year before it was made into a reality show, so you would often still come across guys who'd deploy its techniques, like "negging" you with a gentle insult, totally unselfconsciously. The T-shirt-and-blazer guy went on to tell me about his job "in finance." I excused myself by saying that I had to go home to Brooklyn, which was true. I'd promised my boyfriend that I'd see him play a show that night at a coffeehouse performance space in Bushwick called Goodbye Blue Monday. That, technically, was where I belonged.

But as I bade farewell to the photographer and the author of the book the party was for, I felt the buzzy partyish energy and sense of purpose begin to drain away. A few minutes after I collected my coat from the attendant—without tipping; there was no obvious receptacle and it seemed too weird to fumble for a crumpled bill—and left the bright loft, I was sitting alone in a grimy subway tunnel, absently turning the pages of a magazine. The pictures registered slightly, but I'd absorbed much too much information already that day to even begin to read the words.

As the train headed out of the tunnel and onto the Williamsburg Bridge, I closed the magazine and looked out the window at the borough I was leaving and started writing the post in my head. Nothing too mean about the author, whom I liked, nor her friends, so whom could I safely mock? The rich people for being rich, I supposed, and the heiress-by-marriage for talking about lactation.

And the finance guy, for wearing a stupid shirt and for being a tool and for working in finance. And myself, for being intimidated by a party held in a rich person's home. Easy. I would race through it and get on to the next thing. I was getting better and better at cranking these things out, better and better at scanning a room or a page and isolating the appropriate things to hate. I was eager for it to be tomorrow already, so I could sit down at my desk and start racing through the day again. I wondered if the finance guy would read the post and recognize himself. He'd thought he'd just been hitting on some ordinary girl! He'd been such an idiot.

Joseph's band had been scheduled to be the first band on a bill of seven, kicking off a show that was meant to start at ten, and when I walked in I thought I might have missed them. There was a counter on one side of the room, and the rest of the space was full of old school-room desks, sprung couches, and folding chairs. Dog-eared paperbacks and toys cluttered the room and lined the walls; the eyes of dirty teddy bears stared from the ceiling, from which the bears hung suspended. Every-where there were sweaty young people. It was hard to get out of the habit of scanning a room for things to hate. I rolled up the sleeves of my black dress to make sure that at least a shadowy edge of tattoo showed, feeling stupid for doing this but doing it anyway. I didn't know anyone here. When I'd walked into the book party, seven or eight faces had looked immediately familiar. I scanned the crowd for Joseph.

He was easy to spot with his shaved head and tall, broad-shouldered frame and thick glasses, which is not to say that there weren't several men in the room with an almost identical look. Joseph sometimes referred to Williamsburg as "the hall of mirrors." But he was the tallest and, in my eyes, the most attractive of the cadre of doppel-hipsters. I reached up to brush my lips against his scruffy cheek, but he was distracted, nervous about playing. I asked him when he thought the band would go on, and he said he didn't know. I wished him luck and wandered off toward the bar-counter, where I ordered a hot cider, unspiked because I lived in terror of waking up too hungover to file my first post by nine. He went over to sit with the other members of his band, their heads conspirational and close as they hunched over their beer cans.

A band that wasn't Joseph's went on, filling the room with highly amplified electro-acoustic noise. The band members punched buttons on machines and manipulated pedals to make high-pitched whines and repetitive beeping loops, which was even less fun to watch than it was to listen to. Regular attendance at this kind of show had long been an occupational hazard of being Joseph's girlfriend. I did think he was inventive and talented, but sometimes when I listened to his band or a band like it noodle into another extended car-alarmish solo, I'd find myself thinking about how unfair it was that, even though thousands of people read Gawker, Joseph refused ever to be one of them. He thought the site was shallow and vile.

It was eleven, and then it was midnight, and still Joseph's band showed no sign of being about to go on. I was so bored that I was flipping pages in a faded paperback that I'd found in one of the piles, squinting to see by the greenish-yellow stage light, when Joseph found me and told me that the bill's order had been reversed: his band was now headlining. They would play last. He was still nervous, but I could also tell that he was proud, and happy, and excited. I sighed, exasperated, and told him I was leaving. "You're what?"

"I'm leaving!"

He couldn't hear me over the squawking, so we headed outside. I explained that I had to get up for work in less than six hours, that I wanted to see him play, but that I was tired and couldn't imagine sitting through much more. He listened patiently and when I was done he got out his phone and called a car service, and then he stood and waited with me for the car to come. I kissed him good-bye. I couldn't tell whether he was mad, but right then I was too tired to care.

It would be another half a year or so before Joseph and I broke up, but when we did I kept thinking back to that night, I think because everything that happened between us after it was epilogue. The moment I got into that car, we were done. I should have stayed, of course, and seen him play. But—and this isn't the cop-out thing people always say to excuse their mistakes about how all their experiences have made them who they are and so they have no regrets—I don't know that I would stay, if I could choose, now, to have done so.

I can look back and recognize the things I've done and said that were wrong: unethical, gratuitously hurtful, golden-rule-breaking, et cetera. Sometimes the wrongness was even clear at the time, though not as clear as it is now. But I did these things because I felt the pull of a trajectory, a sense of experience piling up the way it does as you turn the pages of a novel. I would be lying if I said I was a different person now. I am the same person. I would do it all again.

1

Flower

The bulging plastic sheath of cookie dough was nestled obscenely in the cupholder of Phillip's Honda Civic hatchback. I pulled off a chunk: it was still cold. It hadn't been very long, maybe half an hour, since Jon Strass had taken it out of the fridge as we breezed through his empty-after-school house. This was just the kind of debonair playboy lifestyle Jon Strass led: he could come home, grab a tube of chocolate chip cookie dough from the fridge, and take it up to his room to eat with a spoon before (and even a little bit *while*) being deflowered by an older girl from swim team, then run off to play with his friends from the neighborhood, leaving the girl to find her own way home. You had to admire his chutzpah. Also: his centerfold torso, his dick through his Speedo. "You act like you're fourteen years old, everything you say is so obnoxious funny true and mean," I sang along to Liz Phair in Phillip's car. The lyric made me think of Jon, not least because he actually was fourteen years old.

Well, I was only seventeen; it wasn't like what I'd done was *illegal*. It was just wrong, and also it was crazy. "And not in that 'Oooh, you're so crazy!' fun way," Phillip said. "Like, in fact you *are* crazy." He took his eyes off the road and leaned toward me. "Also, you are even more nuts if you think people aren't going to find out about it. *Luke* is going to find out about it. Are you prepared for that to happen?"

"Okay, thank you for coming to pick me up," I said, and turned to stare out the window. We were driving past our high school. On the outside it was all brand-new featureless red brick, like a prison or a mall. On the inside it was more like a mall, with three tiers built overlooking a big main-drag stretch of hallway. Three thousand people went to school there with us. Phillip was right that some substantial percentage of them would eventually hear about what I had done. I was not into thinking about that right then. I beamed out at the blank walls of Montgomery Blair and sang to them, with Liz, about wanting someone's dick "jamming slamming ramming in me."

Phillip sang along too. Phillip would have fucked Jon Strass in a heartbeat. We looked at each other and smiled. "So," he said. "Come on, tell me, I know you want to."

"Hmm?"

"Ha, come on. You know. How was it?"

I described the scene to Phillip the same way I would later describe it in my diary, the same way I described it to myself in my head while it was happening, with florid details and thoughts and feelings cribbed from song lyrics or movie sex scenes. In real time, I mostly only thought about how the Strasses' house smelled. Four people lived there: Jon, his older brothers, and their mom. But her presence seemed incidental: the house looked like a fortress for teenage boys, or a shrine to them. Their sports laundry spilled from duffel bags in the hallways, full of the smell of detergent and their sweat. Overpowering this smell was the scent of pine, rising from the floorboards or from the crushed needles in the yard outside. It wasn't artificial, like Pine-Sol or something: it was the smell of warm sap. It was almost disgustingly sexual. It was a too-symbolic detail, the kind this story is full of, starting with the tube of cookie dough.

Phillip and I spent a lot of time in his car. Sometimes we'd go into DC, to all-ages shows at the Black Cat or to this one café where we smoked cigarettes and ran into people Phillip somehow vaguely knew. Sometimes we'd just go to a particular Wendy's on Rockville Pike whose drive-through window was open late. We were always a little disappointed to arrive at these destinations.

Phillip would pick me up—I had given up on getting my license after denting the minivan's fender on a pylon during my third time failing the road test—and we would turn on the radio or a tape that we would sing along to, competing to drown each other out as we slipped across five lanes of deserted nighttime highway. We sang Bikini Kill and Sleater-Kinney and Stevie Nicks and Rainer Maria and the Rondelles and Tuscadero, but as senior year was drawing to a close, we more and more listened to Liz Phair, who knew how we felt, or told us how to feel if we didn't know.

She knew what it was like to be frustrated about living with people you hated, what it was like to be pressured to perform, to impress. But most of all she knew how important sex was, how it felt to need it, how necessary and urgent a crush could feel. We'd known, of course, that people besides us felt these ways—we had read a lot of books and watched a lot of movies and TV shows. But most of the time the girls in these stories were trying to avoid sex and were loath to leave their parents' protection. And if anyone in these stories was a boy who wanted to fuck other boys, he was usually a sidekick or a red herring, like that swing-dancing dude Cher tries to date in

Clueless. Liz gave us permission to do stupid things and consider them adventures. She sang about trying to fix the car she'd totaled while high "with a rake for a crowbar" in a song called "Stuck on an Island." You could make mistakes and grow up to consider them funny. You could be imperfect and obviously horny and you could sing wrong notes sometimes and you could still be, in your way, important. "Heal my disgust into fame and watch how fast they run to the flame," went the end of the prayer—"Help Me Mary"—that was the second song on her first album. Liz's prayer had worked for her. We sang along so loud. We hoped it would work for us, too.

The future was uncertain. My future was particularly uncertain. That winter we'd all gotten our thick and thin envelopes from different colleges and even Phillip, who got straight Ds in spite of and because of his unique ADD-addled brand of brilliance, had fared better than me. I had been sure that my sweet boyfriend Luke and I would end up together at the artsiest Ivy, since I'd spent four years engineering my transcripts and my life in that direction. But so had a lot of the other thousand people I was graduating with—we went to a magnet school full of groomed overachievers who larded their résumés with titles like "Assistant Treasurer of the Model UN." Luke got into Brown early decision. I got into one school, a safety in Ohio that I hadn't even bothered to visit before deciding to apply.

The fact that this was the worst thing that had ever happened to me says a lot about how smooth-edged my life had been up until this point. I'd thought that I was smart, that it was my smartness that made me exceptional. Now I had to adjust my thinking in one of two ways.

1. I wasn't smart, but something else made me exceptional.
2. I was neither smart nor exceptional.

Option 3, a Zen combination of "college admissions are not the ultimate referendum on your worth as a human being" and "everybody is smart in different ways," didn't occur to me until years later.

This is all by way of explaining that I was in a weird place that spring. I'd tried so hard to be good. I'd seen that being good was ineffective, at best. And also, every single thing happening in my brain and body was about sex and the complicated constellation of gratification feelings clustered around sex that, because I was a girl, I had taught myself to call "love."

Luke and I had mutually lost our virginity in a deliberate, ceremonial way just after my sixteenth birthday, and since then we'd had sex exactly thirteen times. I romanticized everything we did to each other in my diary, fluffing it and surrounding it with semi-plagiarized curlicues. But at swim practice, four days after receiving the last of my thin envelopes (wait-listed by Sarah Lawrence, which had accepted Phillip), I was letting myself think qualitatively about our sex life.

The team was doing a drill with foam pull buoys wedged high between our thighs as we swam on our backs, undulating our hips to make our entire bodies shimmy in a dolphin wave. Whenever I got tired at swim practice I would habitually remind myself of something I felt humiliated or upset about. The flush of anger would translate into a rush of adrenaline, and I'd suddenly have the energy to push through those last few meters to the wall. I didn't feel angry at Luke, exactly, but I did feel shortchanged. I wondered how people managed to do what we'd been doing over and over again throughout their whole lives when, thirteen times in, I felt like we'd exhausted all of the act's possibilities. Luke tried so hard; if there had been AP sex he would have taken it, and aced it, and made sure the credential was in his folder at the guidance office, the way he'd done with the test scores and recommendation letters—so similar to mine!—that had ushered him into his certain, solid future. I clutched the pull buoy harder and rushed closer to the bubbly wake of the girl in front of me.

Practice ended with sprints. We formed lines arbitrarily behind the starting blocks and the coach shouted, "Take your marks . . . GO!" and then people jumped in and raced against each other in nonsensical combinations: tall senior boys against scrawny freshmen, star athletes against halfhearted paddlers who would spend the weekend's meet on the sidelines.

At each "GO!" the line of divers sent up smacking splashes that resounded off the walls of the big, tiled room. I was in line behind an unfamiliar blond boy, a freshman. As he stepped to the block inches in front of me, part of my brain automatically rehearsed the mechanics of my dive while the other part idly registered the smooth tapering of his back from his shoulders down to the pert, squared-off globes of his ass. Then he coiled into his crouch and suddenly his ass was a few inches from my face. I could have reached out and traced the whorls of blond hair that licked up the insides of his thighs.

"Take your marks . . . GO!" shouted the coach, and then the boy was slicing his way through the murky water toward the other end of the pool. As I climbed up to the block, he clambered out of the water at the other end, smiling because he'd won. I could see the outline of his dick clearly from twenty-five meters away and it was as thick as my wrist. I think this was the moment when I first realized that saying you got "weak in the knees" because you were attracted to someone could be a euphemism.

Afterward, the showers were crowded with girls and full of steam and the smell of Herbal Essences and chlorine. Everyone kept her suit on. I borrowed a pink conditioner bottle from someone and rubbed some into my chlorine-bleached split ends while my furtive gaze tracked over the girls' slippery bodies, their razor-burned inner thighs, their breasts pancaked by tight Lycra, their nipples hard against the water's spray. I wanted to be and/or to fuck everything attractive in the world, and it was a light-headed, irrational feeling that I would have thought was like being drunk or high if I'd ever been drunk or high before.

The unspoken understanding was that we weren't going to drive directly home either to my or Phillip's house. Instead we drifted around the neighborhood, cutting up random streets and getting as lost as we could in the sub-division grids and lanes and cul-de-sacs. Phillip rolled down his window to smoke a cigarette and the air that came in was chilly but smelled just slightly of mud and grass, the melting that signaled spring. "Our last spring here," he said, like he'd read my mind.

"Our last everything here. Thank God," I said. I motioned for him to pass me the cigarette and I took a halfhearted, poseurish drag, then reached for the cookie dough to get the taste out of my mouth. Now my fingers smelled like latex, sugar, and nicotine.

"I can't wait to visit you in New York."

"Well, in Bronxville, really."

"Still, it's near New York."

"I can't wait to visit you in Ohio." He smirked. Then he saw my face. "Maybe it'll be unexpectedly awesome," he said apologetically.

"Let's forget that's even happening, tonight." I said. The tape of *Exile in Guyville* was wrapping up, the long slow fade of the last song on the album twanging to a bittersweet, minor-key conclusion. We sailed to the top of a hill, and when we got there we had a long prospect of identical '50s Sears-catalogue houses receding into the distance on either side of the road. Above them the sky was big and suburban, unmarred except by purple sunset clouds. Phillip punched the preset button for the classic rock station and Fleetwood Mac came on, singing about how time casts a spell on you but you don't forget.

The next morning I felt eyes on me as I walked down the hall, and it wasn't my imagination—girls were staring and whispering as I passed. Things were feeling surreal and heightened anyway, so this was just the icing. It was bad television: being dagger-stared by half the people I passed felt familiar, even though it had definitely never happened to me before. When I got to my locker Luke was standing there waiting for me, and instead of initiating a rote morning make-out session he grimaced and shook his head. He took me by the hand and led me through a door to a corridor off the main hallway.

Luke was cute, not handsome, but adorable, like a basset hound puppy. He had wide, pretty eyes and a long nose and a sweet, tender mouth. Even when enraged there was something about his face that was just *funny*. Rage looked out of place when expressed by his amiable features. He had heard what I'd done, he told me, his voice trembling, and he wanted to work past it. He understood that I was going through a rough time right now. We had meant so much to each other, he said, and a note of pleading entered his voice. He was angry but he'd get over it. We only had a few months left to be together, and we should try to make the best of them.

Poor Luke! I wanted to comfort him, but when I reached out to touch his arm he flinched and looked disgusted. I looked into his deep, doggy eyes as I tried to figure out what I could possibly say that might make him feel better. For our two-year anniversary he had given me a photo album full of souvenirs of our relationship, including ticket stubs from movies we'd seen on dates, each meticulously pasted onto its own page and given a funny handwritten caption. How could any apology ever be enough, given these circumstances? What could I say? So I just stood there, saying nothing.

I couldn't get in touch with Phillip the next time I found myself stranded at Jon's house. This was the last time Jon and I ever hooked up. In spite of my attempts to make the things we were doing seem normal by putting a framework of, like, "dating" around them—movie dates, phone calls, all initiated by me—the reality of the situation was crudely poking through. That afternoon we had watched anime from the living room couch while I squeezed his perpetually half-hard dick through his sweatpants and darted intense and, eventually, enraged glances at him. He really was more interested in the cartoons. Well, he was fourteen.

I walked down the street away from Jon's house. His was an older development than the one I lived in; you could tell from the height of the trees that lined the streets. The theory I guess was that I would walk until I hit the main road, at which point I would call Phillip again from a pay phone and if he still wasn't there

I would wait for a bus that would take me at least part of the way home. I could not have called my mom, of course, and I was embarrassed to call any of my other friends. Anyway, I didn't mind the walk; it was clearing my head. It was getting warm out, in the high forties, and that muddy smell of spring was in the air again. It was different from the pine smell. It was smell of damp loamy freshness and budding growth. I felt a surge of irrational happiness.

It was late afternoon and still too cold for kids to be playing outside after school. I walked about a mile without seeing a single person or even being passed by a single car. I felt the vacuum of the empty suburbs surrounding me like a black hole in which my body was suspended, as though I were the only warm alive thing left in the world.

2

The Koi Pond

On 13th Street near Third Avenue recently I passed a long-haired, vaguely Native American–looking guy on the sidewalk and we had this brief awkward moment of eye contact in passing. Why? I wondered. And then a few steps later I remembered in a flash that I had been inside his apartment eight years before, the summer I moved to New York, back when I lived in this neighborhood. "Excuse me, are you an actress?" he'd said to me one day in Kim's Video on Avenue A. Kim's Video on Avenue A, like most video stores, no longer exists. That space, on that block one block west and two blocks south of where I lived five apartments ago, has been at least three different restaurants since it last rented videos. Also, there's a high-rise hotel full of European tourists on Allen between Houston and Stanton now. Really, there are an almost infinite amount of differences, both tiny and enormous, between how things were in the East Village that summer and how things are in the East Village now, but also there are a lot of things—the grimy inexplicable soft-serve place on Avenue A with the handwritten signs in its window, Odessa Bar, the mosaic tile embedded in the sidewalk on the corner of 5th Street—that are still the same, and this makes the differences even more jarring. The city doesn't age in a gradual way like a person. It's like if you ran into someone you'd known eight years ago and he was wearing the same outfit you'd last seen him in but he had gotten so much plastic surgery that you could barely recognize his face.

The long-haired guy looked exactly the same as he'd looked on the day he asked me whether I was an actress. "Sort of," I'd replied, the way probably any nineteen-year-old who'd just moved to New York would, the way probably every nineteen-year-old he ever asked this question of did. Then as now, it was impossible to determine his age. His long hair was glossy dark black and his brown skin was smooth, though his eyeballs were hidden between doubled epicanthic folds above and hound-doggish bags underneath. He was not exactly what you would call attractive. But he radiated—he still radiates—this thing, this almost-charisma. It might be just a sense of permanently belonging to this place, like Odessa Bar or the mosaic tiles. In Kim's Video seven years ago it made him interesting to me because more than anything I wanted that quality of casual familiarity. I had lived in New York for about nine weeks. I told him I had acted in some plays in college, which was true, and he said he was a director, he was casting a movie. I should give him my phone number. I did. I don't remember whether I let him lead me to his section of the store—the videos in Kim's were organized into sections by director—or not.

There's this weird quality of being suspicious and cynical about everything and simultaneously, unwittingly, being utterly open and receptive and gullible that is part of youth, or at least was part of my youth. Circa this incident I would sometimes say to guys in bars who were hitting on me, "Do you know how old I am?" as if, upon finding out, they'd be *ashamed of themselves*. I got hit on in bars a lot because I worked in one. Most of the time I felt like all men were trying to victimize me in some way, and also that this was a compliment. But at the same time I wanted to believe that this guy saw something in me that no one else had yet seen. That from this moment on my life would be transformed. Hadn't this happened, in fact, and in almost this exact same way, to Chloë Sevigny? And now look at her! Eating chicken paprikash at the counter five stools down from me at Veselka, but surrounded by this hush, this almost palpable aura of stardom. Yes, I was the next Chloë Sevigny. Every Spanish-speaking delivery boy on the street knew it somehow, every homeless man playing chess in Tompkins Square Park knew it: they told me I was beautiful every day.

Like many people, I had come to New York City with this idea that I was somehow extraordinary. The important part wasn't "extraordinary," it was "somehow"—I wasn't quite sure what kind of renown it was, exactly, that I was destined for. I just knew that I was really good at *something,* or that I could be, if I could just figure out *what.* Free-floating ambition is toxic because it means that anyone who has accomplished anything in any realm of human endeavor is the enemy because she might be your competition. So you hate everyone a little bit, but behind this wall of hatred you still feel vulnerable. And you *are* vulnerable, but not because of the competition. You're vulnerable because if anyone points you in anything that seems like a direction, that's where you'll go.

In our kitchen, I asked my roommate Claudine what I should do about the director, who had called the number I'd given him to ask me to come over to his apartment and audition. He'd even made a joke about how suspect this sounded: "I'm not a serial killer, I promise. It's just that all my equipment is here." I explained this to Claudine as she made coffee by putting a third of a can of Chock Full o'Nuts grounds in a filter that slotted into a dollar-store plastic holder, then pouring hot water through that into a coffee-stained Pyrex measuring cup underneath. She was wearing two antique slips held together by safety pins and hideous/beautiful brown-and-green chunky-heeled Miu Miu loafers, last season's, bought at a Japanese designer consignment store. She wasn't wearing—does not as a general policy wear—underpants. That summer she was reading a lot of Judith Butler and Proust, and not for school, even though she was designing her own major.

Claudine shrugged and sat down with a teacup full of viscous coffee at our kitchen table, which constituted the entire common space of the apartment. This was where we spent most of our time that summer, endlessly drinking that terrible coffee and writing stories—okay, we wrote one story—and smoking and sculpting miniature food out of plastic clay and eating makeshift meals and listening to the Magnetic Fields *69 Love Songs* on a boom box propped precariously on a shelf above the table. There were a lot of these flimsy plywood shelves on the walls of the kitchen, which, like the rest of the apartment's tiny rooms, was about twice as deep as it was wide. It had one window that looked out across the air shaft directly into the kitchen of our next-door neighbors, with whom we necessarily had a semi-intimate relationship. Claudine lit a Lucky Strike, took a drag, then balanced the cigarette on the edge of her saucer. "I don't know, I mean, I've never heard of this guy, but he says he isn't a serial killer."

It was that simple.

I trusted Claudine's opinion. It was thanks to Claudine, after all, that I was even living in the living room of this East Village two-bedroom railroad apartment. A few months prior I had come to stay with Claudine on a break from classes at Kenyon College in Ohio, where I was finishing up my sophomore year.

Things at Kenyon had not been going particularly well for me, and New York City was a revelation. I remember marveling at the beauty and exciting bustle of filthy Penn Station. I got a disfiguring new hairstyle at a salon I'd read about in *Paper* magazine that was located in the back of a store full of clothes that no one at Kenyon, where the J.Crew delivery truck unloaded metric tons of corduroy and peacoat wool at the tiny post office daily, would even have recognized as garments. I bought as many of them as I could afford and headed back to Ohio, where things continued not to go well despite the fact that I was now, by some definition, a redhead. Then I got a call from Claudine explaining that her roommate was moving out and that she and her other roommate were looking for a replacement. A few days later the spring semester ended and my parents came to pick me up from school in their minivan. Looking out the minivan's window at the manicured cornfields that surrounded Kenyon's towers, I had an internal cinematic good-bye scene: Good-bye cornfields. Good-bye cow pasture. Good-bye Psi Upsilon lodge. I will never see you again.

The director's apartment was on 6th Street between A and B, near the best community garden in the East Village. I had been going to this garden a lot that summer to sit and watch the fish swimming around in the koi pond. They were beautiful and improbable-seeming, these foot-long fish flashing their gleaming, complicated armor in a tiny pool in the center of a city block. There was a tree house in that garden with a balcony from which you could look down at the pond, imagining it was yours, imagining this was your view from your apartment on

East 6th Street in the East Village of New York City, all yours.

The view from the windows of the director's bedroom was similar, maybe better because it was higher up, on the fourth floor of a tenement building. But from this height you couldn't see the fish, only the sun glinting off the surface of the water. We stood there awkwardly, looking out the window, and then he gestured to the bed, which had a thick black bedspread and a wooden futon frame. "I'm sorry it's the only place to sit. I'm just gonna go set up the camera."

As he puttered in the little anteroom off the kitchen, I marveled at the apartment. It had clearly been his for a while. There were built-in bookshelves full of records and books and movies, and stacks of even more movies cluttered the floor. There were framed movie posters on the wall—I recognized *Blow-Up* even though it was in Italian, from the iconic illustration of the splayed woman and the photographer crouching over her. There was a beaded curtain separating the bedroom from the entrance hall and a dusty, overheated smell, a variation on the smell we had in the apartment I shared with Claudine, but this was tempered by the filmmaker's own smell, a not-unpleasant sandalwood-type odor that seemed to emanate from his long, glossy hair. I hadn't been in many apartments yet, or really any apartments that weren't inhabited by NYU students. Once, years ago, I'd visited friends of my parents' family in their brownstone duplex on Joralemon Street in Brooklyn Heights, and I'd felt sorry for them because they had to live in an apartment, whereas my family had a whole house. Now I knew better.

I could see the back of his head and the hair from my perch on the edge of the bed and I tried for a minute to imagine what it would be like to bury my face in it or to run my hand through it. I didn't feel repulsed, exactly.

He returned with a sheaf of typewritten paper and a bulky video camera on a tripod. "Okay, you're Sarah, and I'll read David's lines. Just, you know, be natural . . . I'm not looking to cast someone really studied and polished. I just think you have a good energy."

The compliment warmed and loosened me slightly. But as I began to read the lines of the script the director had written, I felt myself stiffening up, acting. I could tell from the expression on his face that I wasn't doing well, which made me try harder, which made my acting worse. After we'd gone through a few pages of the script he turned off the camera. "Do you want a drink or something? You seem really nervous."

I said yes, please, a beer, and could I use his bathroom. I didn't have to go, but I wanted to see what an adult man's bathroom would look like. I'd seen sinks full of stubble and dried phlegm lumps in boys' shared dorm bathrooms, and in the bathroom of the squalid ranch house that one of my Kenyon boyfriends had shared with four of his frat brothers. I wanted to see what would be in the director's medicine cabinet but I didn't want him to hear the click of its opening, so instead I contented myself with sniffing his towels and taking a long time to wash my hands with the black soap that sat in its own little bamboo holder. Washing my hands with his soap seemed so intimate. When I stepped out of the bathroom he handed me a Kirin, and even though I'd been to a college that basically offered a minor in alcohol consumption, the afternoon beer seemed exotic.

We sat at the director's kitchen counter, drinking, and he told me a little bit more about the plot of the movie. Basically Sarah is a young beautiful waitress and David is an older married businessman whose life has been pretty boring and he's never experienced anything remotely like a grand passion. When he unexpectedly gets fired from his deadening job, he feels like he can't tell his wife, so he keeps commuting into the city every day but instead of his office he goes to the diner where Sarah works and nurses a cup of coffee there all day. Sarah is quirky, which means she is given to wearing one loud accessory at all times, like a feather braided into her hair. Eventually she notices David and asks him what's going on, and he tells her, and together they hatch a plan to get him his job back by blackmailing the CEO, whose dirty secrets Sarah knows because her terrible abusive boyfriend is a drug dealer. Eventually of course Sarah and David realize they belong together, and they don't belong here in this terrible town, and so together they embark on a series of hijinks via which they defeat the shady CEO and the abusive boyfriend and the forgotten wife and ride off into the sunset, fully alive for the first time. While he told me about all this I nodded politely and fake-laughed and looked rapt, even though it was the dumbest thing I'd ever heard.

My second attempt at reading the script was better, but not by much. After the director turned off the camera we both stood up and started moving toward the door, and the slowly building suspicion that he was not going to put the moves on me finally crystallized into certain knowledge. He said he would be in touch about the role sometime in the next couple of weeks, and then he leaned in and gave me a slight, uncomfortable half-hug, and brushed my cheek with his dry, purplish lips.

It was the moment I could have given him the go-ahead by leaning in just a few inches, by just very slightly pressing my breasts into the flat, featureless plank of his torso. I would have been doing it out of curiosity, and to salve my slightly wounded ego or to replace that wound with another kind. I recognized the moment. A few weeks earlier I'd wound up sleeping with a boy, a friend of Claudine's with crooked teeth and a goatee, the kind of person who wore tweed hats and used the word *bohemian* in self-descriptive earnest. I had just been idly flexing the muscle of my charm to prove to myself that it was there, and then suddenly we were past the point of nonawkwardly turning back.

I'd made all these enthusiastic noises during the sex in order to convince myself that I was enjoying it, which was something I did a lot back then. In the morning he was full of swagger and I was totally repulsed, filled with that strange feeling of having somehow molested myself.

This time, with the director, I didn't lean in. I walked down the stairs and out into the sunlight on 6th Street, as safe, I guess, and as innocent as I'd been walking in.

Sometimes I wonder how I survived that first summer in New York without getting cracked like an egg on the pavement.

I also wonder if there was some moment when men began to sense that the skepticism I'd once feigned had calcified into something real, and so they stopped trying to sway me. Or maybe they don't sense anything and they just see that I'm almost a decade older now. And anyway the streets and the bars are full of easier prey: girls whose eyes, behind their sunglasses, are filled with this targetless, nameless need.

3

World of Blues

When I came in to World of Blues in the late afternoon I'd go straight into the back room and fill up a big bucket with almost equal parts Murphy Oil Soap and water and bring it out to the bar. The chairs and tables were scrambled wherever they'd been left the night before and it was my job to line up the tables and turn the chairs so they all faced the stage. Then I would wipe down the tables with the soap-water from my bucket, so that the tangy antiseptic smell of the soap could cut through the fermented alcoholic stink that oozed from the upholstered banquettes and the velvet curtains and the wooden floorboards and especially from the unstop-pered bottles in the well of the bar, tucked away just out of sight.

Next I would shake out about half a bag of ground coffee into the giant urn in the back room and fill the hopper with cold water and switch it on, after which the acrid smell of soap and booze and coffee would settle over the bar, wafted by the AC. Sara would pick a place to order dinner from—big platters of pasta, usu-ally, or sandwiches or fried chicken—and open up the till and give me some money to get lemons and limes at the grocery store up the block, and sometimes matches or gum or cigarettes from the convenience store across the street if we needed them. Then she would slice the fruit as I scraped the old wax from the candleholders and plopped new little votive candles inside them until our dinner arrived. When it did we would fill up pint glasses with seltzer and cranberry from the soda gun and take them to one of the front tables so we could stare out the window as we ate. People walked by in shorts and sundresses and sunglasses. We wore low-rise jeans, sneakers, and tank tops that showed our bra straps. No one had told us to, it was just understood to be the uniform.

We talked about our lives outside the bar and wolfed the rich food. Everything was quiet and sunny and cozy. Then ten more minutes passed and we had to turn on the music and draw the curtains and unlock the door, and from then on the night could go a couple of different ways.

It was the summer of 2003, my third summer in New York; I was twenty-one, and I had gotten a job by answering a Help Wanted ad in the *Village Voice*. When I first moved to New York, and then even still after I'd been living in New York for a couple of years, I held a series of jobs that I found by answering these classified ads, just a few pages away from the notorious ass-cheek–filled ads catering to the needs of the apparently huge New York population whose back pain can only be soothed by the massaging hands of a pre-op transsexual. There are a lot of ways to get a service job, especially now that the Internet exists (it did then too, but less so), and answering a newspaper ad, I would eventually come to realize, is among the worst. But I did it, and kept on doing it, out of a strange conviction that I would be provided with some awesome opportunity because of my sheer pluck and luck and skill at being myself. People who are new to New York often suffer this kind of delusion; the same stripe of hopeful, literal-minded credulity my visiting mom exhibits when she sees an awning advertising "Famous Best Sandwiches" decorating some dime-a-dozen bodega and wonders aloud why we don't go in and try one.

The ad said that World of Blues offered a competitive salary and a fast-paced, friendly environment, with lots of room for advancement. Experience was preferred, but not necessary. Every single one of those things should have announced itself to me as a big red flag, and I wasn't so dense that I didn't vaguely suspect this to be the case. But I missed, or chose to ignore, the biggest and reddest flag of all: all summer long, that ad was running in the weekly paper each time that paper was published.

All of the bartenders were pale and thin but Sara, my favorite, was the palest and thinnest, with the downy kind of light-brown hair that's so fine and limp it always looks slightly dirty. A fleshy mole on her chin kept her face from being perfect, but her silhouette was prettiest behind the bar, miniature and graceful, with round, perfect breasts that she hunched to half-conceal, like a slim tree drooping with fruit. She couldn't remember how long she'd been working at World of Blues, which, like all the employees, she called Worst of Blues. "God, three years maybe? Yeah, because I remember right before I started it was my twenty-fifth birthday." She had finished college and she wasn't trying to be an actress or anything, so it was hard at first to understand what had trapped her.

Two men, David and Don, co-owned the club, but Don seemed to have a much more active role in its management, booking the acts and playing the jovial host on the rare occasion that a musician who wasn't one of our regulars—that is to say, a musician who might bring in customers—came to play a set. The rest of the time, World of Blues's bill was filled with men who spent their days busking in subway terminals around the city, middle-aged men who could noodle out the set of standards that would give a mostly tourist audience a generic Blues Club In New York City experience. They probably played "Sweet Home Chicago" at least ten times during each of my 4 P.M.–to–4 A.M. shifts. Don was in charge of these musicians, too, but his interactions with them were perfunctory, his charm switch set to "off." With the waitresses the charm switch was always on. With the bartenders it varied; most of them had been there so long that he had either given up or had, a word or gesture occasionally hinted, been there and done that. He was in his early thirties, well under six feet tall, and blessed with a smarmy blond symmetry that made possible his side career as an occasional TV-commercial actor. His beautiful wife made rare early afternoon appearances, always seeming slightly disgusted with the place. He talked about her a lot, about how beautiful she was and how much he loved having sex with her. Whether a bartender humored him or subtly grimaced as he did this was one indicator of whether or not she remained on his to-do list. Sara grimaced.

"Watch out for Don," Sara told me on my second day. "But watch out for David more." David was older and hardly ever came into the bar, and when he did it was always near closing time. Sometimes David and Don would hold tense, hushed conversations at the table we kept reserved for them at the end of the bar, near where I picked up my orders. Other times David would be lavishly drunk, his eyes almost closed in his crumpled face, and he'd sit at the special table with a lucky patron or waitress near closing time and shake his long, wet-looking black curls with laughter, refilling everyone's glasses with expensive wine he'd brought with him from home. I hadn't yet been summoned to sit at the table with David.

That night when Sara and I finished eating dinner there were only a few minutes left until we would have to open the door, and we spent them standing just outside the back door, smoking and drinking coffee and watching the sky change color as the heat of the summer day began to dissipate. When we walked back into the front room, Mary was there, tying on her little apron and grinning. She was going to tell us about an audition, I sensed.

"I had the best audition today," Mary said. "Which monologue did you do?" we asked. Instead of answering, she repeated the monologue. I sat down at the owners' table to watch her and she kept her eyes locked on mine the whole time, really selling it.

Mary looked like an ad for Neutrogena face wash, with her laser-whitened teeth the exact shade of the whites of her always-widened eyes. Her low-rise jeans always rode extra low on her long torso; she was a scrupulous waxer. She had a habit of shaking out her glossy brown ponytail from its holder that she tended to deploy mid-monologue or mid-taking-someone's-order. She was the kind of person who hugged everyone hello and good-bye and she seemed genuinely to like her job, which she was inarguably the best at. Every night she got the bonus that went to the waitress who'd racked up the highest sales total, a not inconsiderable forty dollars. Paying whoever was making the most money more money didn't make a lot of sense to me. I was a student at the New School, taking lots of classes whose upshot seemed to be "Here's what's wrong with capitalism," none of which were preparing me very well to go out into it. Mary made sure her sales total was the highest by, if necessary, going into your section after things got crowded and taking the orders of the people you'd been too busy to notice. She would also take orders from people standing near the bar, which the bartenders quietly resented. And though this didn't help her sales total, she would also tell groups of customers who she deemed unlikely to tip—foreign tourists, older women— that the drink prices, which weren't posted anywhere, were a few dollars higher than the already-high prices were. She had explained this to me as she was training me, and I had resolved not to follow suit, and then of course I eventually followed suit.

World of Blues was also the kind of place where you had to order a drink in order to sit at a table, a policy that is a bitch to enforce. "Okay, can I have a seltzer water?" "Sure, that'll be three dollars." "What?" was the conversation you would have with the cheapskates who'd naively thought the ten dollars they'd paid to hear the music would be their final investment in that evening's fun. Mary banished these people without mercy, tapping her feet by their table until they got up to make way for paying customers. She would tolerate couples, but large groups of single men were her favorite. Well, they are every waitress's favorite. You could develop a little relationship with them over the course of the evening, figure out who was paying, have some banter with him, and make eye contact. As long as you didn't then run into him in the unattended hallway on the way back from the bathroom, everything would be fine.

When I'd first started and Mary had been training me, I got the sense that she trained new waitresses pretty often. Now I trained a new girl once every couple of weeks; they never lasted. There was a type of person who could thrive in the job, or maybe there were a couple of types. Mary was one of them: ruthless and sexual, quick to sit on a lap. Her acting career might not have been taking off, but she was good at playing a role. The weirdest thing about her was that she was possessed of one of those nominal Christian Midwestern virginities, still, at twenty-two. She would scold you for taking the Lord's name in vain, which she never did, and she'd say "sugar!" when she spilled something rather than curse. I used to imagine her saying "sugar!" when I opened the door and caught her in Don's office upstairs with her face in his lap, but this never happened.

So the team that night was me, Mary, and Sara, and I had the section near the stage and Mary had the section near the windows in front. If it got packed and there were customers leaning against the railing opposite the bar, and if the bar was three deep and they couldn't make their way over, those people would be fair game for either of us. Another foot closer to the bar and they were Sara's. At five the first performer loaded in and the first few customers came through the door, sniffing around curiously before selecting a table in Mary's section. They had fanny packs and water bottles and glasses: the type you'd have to force to order soda. It would probably be hours before anyone sat in my section, so I went to the back room to talk to Devil Redbone while he unpacked his gear.

Devil Redbone was an amiable finger-picker in his fifties, a dad from New Jersey whose talent was to play and sing blues standards with such technical skill and such a fluid, familiar style that our customers rarely noticed he was there. The smooth baritone and guitar licks could have been emanating from the PA, not the flannel-shirted man at the front of the room. He often played the first set, when customers were few and far between, and he must have taken the job just to hear himself sing. One of the waitresses' duties was to carry a silver champagne bucket marked "Tips" around the room at the end of each set, a panhandlerish gesture that, combined with the cover charge and inflated drink prices, must have struck customers as downright extortionate. When there were only three or four occupied tables in the place it also seemed ridiculous, but we did it anyway for Devil, whose actual name was Rob.

When he'd finished tuning his guitar, Devil and I poured ourselves cups of coffee from the big urn and sat on milk crates by the back door. The sky was almost navy now, and the greasy garlic smell of the bad red-sauce Italian places up and down the block was blowing through the backyards, borne by powerful restaurant exhaust fans. "Sometimes I think about what this neighborhood used to be, why these tourists all come here with their

maps, thinking they're going where the artists hang out,"
Devil said. "Like they're going to fall through a hole in
the space-time continuum and come into a place like this
and Bob Dylan will be here, and Suze Rotolo will be
serving drinks in a leotard." A minute later I peeked out
the swinging doors of the back room and saw a couple
arranging themselves on one of the banquettes in my section. Mary was swanning across the room toward them
but I banged through the doors with Devil behind me.
He rushed to the stage as I rushed to the table. Mary
pretended that she had been heading over to straighten
the votive candles that I'd arranged in the front rows. It
wasn't that I wanted the couple's two dollars, or even
that I wanted to defend my territory. I just wanted to
be functional. You had to start getting into a groove as
early as possible in the night, get used to a certain kind of
interaction so that later, when it was busy, the requisite
facial expressions and banter and elementary arithmetic
would come to you automatically.

I went over and talked to the couple, addressing myself primarily, as I used to think I should, to the woman.
She was my age or a little bit older, with dyed red curly
hair that caught the red and blue stage lights. "What can
I get you guys?" I asked her. "Double Stoli Vanilla and
Diet Coke and a Heineken," the man told me. He was
thirtyish, heavyset, jowly. His pack of Marlboro Lights
and his lighter were out on the table. This was just after

the smoking ban in New York bars had passed and people sometimes tried to press their luck and see if we were one of the places that wouldn't enforce it.

I went over to the bar and put in their order with Sara, poised with my tray and swizzle sticks and a cherry for the cocktail. The next part was the hard part. I returned to the table, set up little napkin homes for the beverages in front of their new owners, gently placed the drinks down, and swiveled the tray around under my arm, then kept my expression blank as I said, "That'll be twenty dollars. Would you like to start a tab?" The jowly man registered the shock semigracefully—nearly every other bar on the block had half-price happy hour specials—and I realized this was a date, because if the redhead had been an established girlfriend he'd have complained. The order itself, the double, should have tipped me off that this was a goal-oriented evening. The couple sat and sipped their drinks and watched Devil Redbone work his way through "Sweet Melissa," sounding more than a little like Darius Rucker. When Joe the bouncer arrived I went outside to say hi.

Joe was this chubby, thick-necked Irish guy who had to put a plain black shirt over the Rancid and NOFX shirts he wore to work so, Don said, the customers wouldn't be confused about what kind of music went on at World of Blues. I liked Joe because he was honest about everything and loved to gossip, though I suspected he had no loyalties and probably talked to the other employees about me the same way he talked to me about them: "I fuckin' hate David," he'd say, or "Mary is such a cunt," and then go on to detail some annoying personal habit or petty grievance. He also seemed genuinely uninterested in having sex with me and, almost incidentally, genuinely interested in protecting me, which impressed me against my will. The closest he'd ever come to flirting with me had been this random languid moment one night around seven when we were both floating around in the foyer of the bar, waiting for things to pick up and watching Sara occupy herself with inventory. He turned to me as I was reaching up overhead to pull my short hair back into a miniature ponytail. "You know, when they first hired you, I didn't get it, but now I see how you could be kind of hot." From another kind of guy this would have been an insult, or the kind of insult that's really a sexual provocation in disguise. From Joe it was a simple observation: he had figured out why someone might think I was attractive, sort of like how he'd figured out that of all the places to get a pizza slice within a three-block radius the place with the cornmeal crust was best, or that a dash of Tabasco in a draft Budweiser made a strangely tasty cocktail. I had thought a few times of bringing Joseph by and introducing him to Joe—they would have hit it off for sure—but I kept somehow not getting around to letting Joseph see what it was like where I worked.

Tonight Joe was agitated. "Fucking Sumpter Pickins. I fucking hate that dude," he muttered. The place will be packed with Long Island assholes who have no idea but want to be part of a crowd and cheap Japanese douche-bags who have his like one rare EP, and he'll shit in his diaper and stink up the back room and nod out halfway through his set."

Sumpter Pickins was an elderly bluesman, some ver-sion of the real thing, and that probably would have awed me if I'd been anything like a blues aficionado. Sumpter was such an authentic bluesman that he was even a lifelong heroin addict, which, I was learning, was a more common condition among elderly or prematurely elderly looking New Yorkers than I had known. From TV and movies you get the impression that all heroin addicts start out hard and glamorous and quickly degen-erate into disgusting pockmarked bums who then either clean up or die, but there are a bunch of pale, vaguely embalmed-looking middle-aged people wandering around lower Manhattan who will tell you otherwise. They just do enough to "maintain" and they almost all just smoke it and only ever have smoked it, which is why they're alive.

Sumpter Pickins definitely had the embalmed look: it was as though someone had thought highly enough of Sumpter Pickins to install him in Madame Tussauds, ex-cept that it was really him. He got around via wheelchair because his feet had been amputated, and Joe was correct that he wore adult diapers. To compensate for his inability to control his bowels he doused himself with an incensey cologne, and the smell this created, huge artificial flowers covering subtle rot, would haunt the back room for days after he played a show. The upside was that he was polite and kind, would tip us for the free sodas we brought him, and was one of the few regulars at World of Blues who had actual fans.

True to Joe's prophecy, by eleven that night we were hitting a sweet spot: Long Islanders and blues nerds alike crammed the tables and were packed tightly along the path I had to walk every time I returned to the bar to pick up more drinks. On one return trip I found Don, who'd been in the backroom kissing Sumpter's ass, behind the bar with Sara, who was getting slammed. Instead of helping her out, though, he was taking a series of bottles down from the quick-draw racks behind the bar and flipping them in the air like Tom Cruise in *Cocktail*, then splashing their contents into a shaker. He'd lined up a row of shot glasses on the bar in front of him. Every time Sara passed him on her way to frantically dig more ice out of the bucket or change another twenty at the cash register, he'd interrupt his tricks to flick her ass playfully with the tip of a bar towel. "Chocolate cake shots!" he finally announced, emerging from behind the bar and placing them on the owners' table. "Oooh, chocolate cake shots!" Mary cooed, slapping down three new tickets for Sara and turning to the table. This was the kind of enthusiasm we were all supposed to feel when one of the owners offered us a drink, because we weren't technically "allowed" to start drinking until a few hours before closing. We always did start earlier, though, especially Sara, whose every drink from her after-dinner coffee on was laced with vodka. I never particularly wanted to start early, because of how tricky it became for me to add up bills and how much longer and more arduous the night seemed to be afterward. Also, chocolate cake shots are disgusting. I drank one. Then I positioned three vodka-cranberries on my tray and walked back into the crowd with the tray balanced above my head.

Onstage, Sumpter Pickins was hitting his stride, his mournful, velvet-lined voice lending undeserved gravitas to (what else?) "Sweet Home Chicago." Parts of the crowd were drunk enough to shout along with the chorus. I dropped off the drinks with a table full of college girls and turned my attention to the guys who'd just sat down next to them. There were five of them clustered around one of the tiny tables, and this was clearly not their first stop of the evening. I opened up my face and innocently asked what I could do for them. "Come sit down and have a drink with us, baby," said a thick-necked guy in a tight T-shirt with a dragon on it. I "laughed." The performance, of course, was for the benefit of dragon-shirt's friends, and if I would collude with him in it, he'd re-ward me. This was what always happened to me, with small variations. I think this is what always happens. The waitress's role is always the same: she's supposed to be a receptive audience for witticisms like "I'd like an order of you." It's a ritual that has almost nothing to do with sex and everything to do with dominance, the dude asserting his place at the head of his pack. It's gross, but what are you supposed to do, give every man who walks into the bar a lecture? In a New School classroom I could talk about gender politics, but at World of Blues, I was there to make money. True, I could have become one of those flies-with-vinegar waitresses; they usually do well, tipswise, because their coldness makes customers eager to win them over. But my instinct in these situations is always to please. I wish I could say this has changed a lot since I was twenty-one.

After that first shot, things blurred and bleared. I brought the table of boys more rounds and gave the dragon-shirted guy more conspiratorial smiles. As the crowd thinned I put wads of ones on the shelf for Lana to change into twenties so that the pouch of my apron wouldn't bulge; I began to close out my credit-card tabs. Don flitted around the room, chatting up the prettier, drunker patrons. The vodka-cranberry girls got a free round, on him, and when I brought it to them he was sandwiched between two of them on the banquette, looking intently into the eyes of a tanned blond who couldn't have been more than a freshman. He was saying he wanted to help her pick a major. Back at the waitress station, David had taken his place at the owners' table, where the champagne bucket we used to collect tips had been filled with ice to cool a slim green bottle. "Ice wine," he told me, catching the direction of my glance. "You must try a glass once you're done with your things." He fluttered a hand in the direction of the back room, where I would count up the money in my pouch, making one stack for the bar and another for myself.

We sat on the couch to do this, Mary being the speediest, flicking twenties into piles of five like a bank teller. I counted and recounted, terrified of making a mistake, then brought my piles to the bar, one to be taken, one to be changed into larger denominations.

As usual, Mary's stacks were the biggest, bigger than mine by at least three piles. Sometimes it seemed like a good idea to shortchange yourself a bit, to make it seem like you'd sold more drinks than you really had. Since you had overcharged your customers, it was easy to feel generous toward the institution that had allowed you to do so. Also, it was always a good idea to tip out the bartender a little more than you had to. And what was left after that still seemed like a terrifying amount of money to walk home with.

A row of cabs waited outside. It was four thirty. And

there was David, at the owners' table, proffering a glass of sickly sweet wine syrup, icy condensation on its bowl ready to liquefy under my hot fingertips.

I took my seat and took a sip. He smiled and I smiled back, my mechanism for friendly interpersonal communication with near-strangers being, at this point in the evening, completely automated.

"So, you like working here?" he asked. I nodded. "You are a student, yes?" I nodded again. "What do you study?" I told him and he launched into a monologue about an author, no one I'd heard of. He segued into a discussion of the beauty of his Mediteranean home country's women, the perfidy of his ex-wife, the merits of the wine we were drinking. I must have murmured a sentence or two, struggling to keep from slurring my words. Since about two I'd been handing Sara my half-full coffee mug and having her fill it the rest of the way up with Baileys and vodka, bringing two half-full mugs of coffee so she could do the same. I noticed suddenly that my feet, in their Converse, were wet—my socks were drenched with a mixture of sweat and spilled beer. I raised the glass of sugary wine back to my lips and felt the warmth of drunken exhaustion, the relief that comes as a wash of adrenaline trickles out of your brain. I tried to participate in the conversation David was having with himself, feeling strained, like a precocious child invited to sit with the adults. I was dimly aware of Mary hugging everyone on her way out, Joe and the Mexican teenager who mopped the floor chugging beers at the deserted bar, Don swaggering up the stairs to the office, a flash of light brown hair on the girl trailing behind him.

The night sky was beginning to glow with daybreak when David finally allowed himself to notice that I was tired. "Sleep well, dear. See you tomorrow," he said as he walked me to the door. And as I turned to face the row of cabs, one of which would bear me down Houston as the sky turned pink, he leaned down and kissed me on the cheek. His hair brushed my face and the spot on my face where his parted lips touched me was wet. His smell clung to me in the cab, the winy sharpness of his saliva making my cheek feel tight and itchy.

"Did you have a good time?" the cabdriver asked. "I did okay, it was pretty busy," I told him, wanting to make sure he knew I was like him: an employee of the night, not another patron.

It wasn't long, maybe a week or two, after that night that I called World of Blues at an hour when I was sure no one would be there so that I could leave a message on their answering machine. "Hi, this is Emily, I'm just calling to say I won't be in for my shift on Thursday. Or actually any shift, ever, because I quit," I said to the answering machine, and then I hung up.

A few days later I ran into Sara on the street. She was walking with her head down and I didn't recognize her until she had almost passed me because her outdoor facial expression was so different from the vocabulary of faces she wore at the bar. She looked happy but wary. I flagged her down and we hugged. "Everyone has been worried about you! Why'd you quit like that?" she asked. I was embarrassed; the gesture of quitting via rude voice mail, which at the time had seemed defiant, now seemed cowardly and immature. It belonged to one of the girls who'd only worked a few shifts with us—the sturdy-thighed modern dancer, the Staten Island teenager who never shut up about her boyfriend—before disappearing, leaving only a faint impression of their extra-bar identities. Already I'd stopped telling the anecdote about quitting to friends in a bragging way and now I told it in a self-deprecating way, if I told it at all.

Sara looked beautiful in a gauzy Marc by Marc Jacobs sundress that was not the kind of thing you'd ever wear in an environment where industrial cranberry juice concentrate and beer might splash on you, so it must have been her night off. I had no idea what to say to her. I didn't want to say anything bad about the bar. It had been okay to complain when we both worked there, but now it seemed like complaining would just underscore the difference between us. That difference had been there since the beginning; she'd probably always known about it. In the next few months I would have two more waitressing jobs and then I would graduate, and then I would temp for three months until I got an office job where for years I would make less money than we'd taken home in stacks of twenties, but at least it would be a daytime job. And I would avoid the block World of Blues was on (which wasn't hard, actually) for years, just in case anyone was having a cigarette out front when I walked by. If it were Don or Joe or David, I wouldn't want them to see me. But if it were Sara, I wouldn't want to see her and know that she was still working there.

But that day, running into Sara on the sidewalk under some scaffolding between First and A, I was happy to see her. After an awkward pause, I figured out how to shrug off the question of why I'd quit—"Oh, you know," I said. "The music was getting on my nerves." We laughed and we told each other we would call each other and make plans to hang out, and we stood in a pool of late summer twilight talking about nothing, parting, finally, in a way that didn't feel like it was the last time.

4

A Concentration in Writing

In the summer of 2001 I interrupted my undergraduate education in order to move to New York. Usually I tell people that I dropped out of Kenyon, but that is an oversimplification slash total lie. The truth is a lot less impressive: rather than sever my ties to school entirely, scandalizing my parents and bidding my high school overachiever identity good-bye forever, I enrolled in this New York internship program, a sort of study-abroad cop-out for people who were sick of Kenyon but not of America. The organization housed Midwestern college students in bunk-bedded rat holes and charged them college tuition to attend weekly meetings about their internship experiences. I moved in with Claudine instead, and I skipped all the meetings. I never ended up getting credit for that semester because by the time it started I had already applied to the New School, which very reasonably wouldn't accept that three months spent taking notes about making Xeroxes equaled three months of class.

When I explain why I "dropped out" of Kenyon I also usually say it was because I "just wasn't into Ohio," and that is also a lie. What I just wasn't into was more complicated, and not the kind of thing I—even I—would tell someone I'd just met.

At Kenyon I had been variously a studio art, a drama, and finally an English major, but the undergraduate part of the New School has no majors, only "concentrations." The only graduation requirements for a "concentration" in writing that I hadn't fulfilled at Kenyon were a bunch of writing workshops, so starting in the spring of 2002 I was in enrolled in one writing workshop or another, and sometimes more than one, continuously until graduation.

My first writing workshop was in a second-floor classroom with windows that faced out onto 12th Street and a long rectangular table with seven girls clustered near one end of it. It was a memoir-writing workshop. The teacher, Beth, looked like the affable grandma on a bag of cookies and had written a series of memoirs about her interracial family. The first prompt she gave us was simple: "I want you to look within and ask yourself this question: 'How am I a victim?'"

I looked within but I couldn't come up with much. In an all-female class, bemoaning the burden of womanhood seemed like an unwise strategy if I wanted to make my story stand out. I sensed that what Beth really wanted was for each of us to claim a label, like "anorexic" or "addict," so that she could slot our stories into that box for the remainder of the semester. I ended up writing a sad essay about how having sex with a female friend at Kenyon during my final semester there had subtly soured our relationship. ("Bisexual.")

The next day I learned that roughly half of the class were real full-time lesbians, or at least were committed to being lesbians for all four years of college. They smirked at my description of my sad morning after with Liz, who had passed on hitting the dining hall together for breakfast, saying that she was busy but would call me later, which she did not do. The essay ended with a description of looking out the car window at the cornfields as my parents' car pulled away from Kenyon for the last time, and the class wasn't having that part, either. "What does the ending have to do with anything?" asked a girl who had the Hebrew word for *writer* tattooed on her inner wrist, and I couldn't explain, because at that time

I sincerely didn't know; it was like a scab had formed around a chunk of my memories, and this girl was right that the elision of these scabbed-over memories had rendered my story meaningless. Her victim story was about being elbowed by a cop at a protest against the World Trade Organization.

The next girl read aloud an essay entitled "Memoirs of an Angry Black Woman Syndrome," It seemed like the author had not reread or checked her story over in any way for basic sentence coherence, and this felt insulting, like being served food the chef hasn't tasted. In terms of victim cred, though, she'd aced the assignment, to the point where it was difficult to believe so many sad things had happened to one person.

Beth was not one of those writing teachers who bother to fake impartiality. "I loved this piece," she told the class, and then we went around in a circle and everyone either else said a reason why they'd loved it too; or just offered sympathy: "That was so sad, the part when your dad left." When it was my turn, I asked a clarification question in a way that made it unnecessarily obvious that I thought the essay was poorly written. Its author narrowed her eyes at me, then kept glaring as her mouth smiled. "I'm sure you're just speaking from ignorance, not racism," she said.

The next semester I opted out of taking another memoir class with Beth and enrolled in a fiction class with

Dot, and it was in this class, for the first time at the New School, that I finally made friends, sort of. Dot's classroom was on the other side of the building, overlooking the central courtyard where, on breaks, we all smoked cigarettes and rehashed the conversations about one another's stories that we'd had during class. Sometimes during class the smell of smoke drifted in through the open windows, further smudging the already-blurry distinction between the life and the work.

Dot was short and wiry, with a wild halo of frizzy gray hair and dark glasses that she wore indoors. She exactly resembled the kind of Roz Chast cartoon character who is always about to say something gloomy or sardonic, but actually in class she hardly said anything. For this, especially post-Beth, I liked her a lot. Everyone in our class, some of whom enrolled in her class every semester, liked her a lot. We tried to get her to like us, too, or to say she liked our stories, but she never did. She would occasionally deliver gnomic little nuggets during critique or scribble something illegible in a margin and we would huddle over that page together in a bar on University after class and try to figure out what she'd written. "It might say 'Gut,' like 'good' but in German? Is she German?" With typical twenty-year-old utter self-absorption we assumed that Dot's reticence was a strategy, crafted to provoke us to new heights of literary achievement by making us compete for attention that she doled out at carefully chosen intervals that only *seemed* random. It never occurred to us to think that maybe she was clocking in and out of her job each day with minimal effort, the same way that we sleepwalked through the filing and faxing and takeout-order-jotting that constituted our nascent working lives.

And that was the problem: we were all getting close to graduating, and the information we were gleaning from internships and part-time jobs was making it hard for us to keep pretending it was possible that we were going to graduate from writing school and somehow become *writers*. That semester I was making five dollars an hour organizing filing cabinets at a publishing house a few blocks away from school. When I was done organizing the cabinets I would be given stacks of unpromising submissions to read. The reader reports I wrote about these submissions were scathing and studiously clever, full of condescending rhetorical questions and parodies of the submissions' worst failings. These reports were also a complete waste of time, full of the misplaced vitriol that feeds on unfocused ambition. In fact the submissions were, for the most part, okay. Some were worse than others, and those were depressing because how sad was it that someone had worked for years to produce a big stack of boring pages? The good ones were depressing too, especially when their quality compared favorably to some of the books the house had recently published. I took those books home to read at the end of a day of filing rejection letters attached to photocopies of cover letters that prominently mentioned Columbia, Syracuse, and Iowa. I imagined those places to be like Dot's class, all the time, for two years. I couldn't decide whether that sounded like fun or like hell.

One time we were workshopping a story by Scarlett, the class's most controversial writer. Even I, with my intern's professional expertise in judging literary talent, still hadn't figured out whether Scarlett was a dumbass or a savant operating on an experimental level the rest of us weren't ready for. Scarlett had been raised a west coast JAP but now had the tattooed forearms, muscular torso, and perpetual trucker hat/fancy sneakers/baggy jeans outfits that were then the uniform of a certain kind of hipster lesbian. The Scarletts of New York were often featured in *Vice* magazine's Do's and Don'ts column, but you didn't have to read *Vice* to know that Scarlett was a Do. She even smelled charismatic, like cigarettes, of course, and Old Spice and unfeminine sweat.

Unlike the rest of us, Scarlett didn't even bother pretending that her stories were about anyone other than Scarlett herself. They were full of rambling descriptions of parties and sad phone calls with lovers and family members, and for some reason their many basic spelling and syntactical errors didn't detract from their allure, or undermine her authority as a narrator. After a quick stab at dealing with the stories as stories, our conversation devolved, as usual, into plain nosiness. The mother character, it was decided, was being unrealistic and bigoted by asking "Violet" not to bring her girlfriend home for Passover, and the drunken fender-bender that their fight had caused was mostly the mother character's fault. That night, the Scarlett discussion was uncharacteristically peaceful for our class. More usually we'd get into fights, with alliances shifting so continuously that none of us could sustain lasting grudges because it was so difficult to keep track of who was on whose side. Dot in her wisdom would sit back and allow these fights to play out to their conclusions, unless possibly she was dozing off. The dark glasses made it hard to tell.

After class my friends and I met up on the sidewalk outside: Me, Scarlett, Calvin, Lana, and Ellen. Ellen and Scarlett were friends, as were Calvin and Lana, and all of these people had been in Dot's class before and had their writerly personae pretty much worked out.

Lana, whose last name was White, wrote memorably icky stories about a character named Ava Black who was always having consensual but patently exploitative sex with men who were a lot older than she was. She was tall and blond, with an overbite and an internship at a literary magazine. She had a knack for saying perceptive, cutting things about your story in a mild tone of voice. I secretly disliked her but obviously we had some things in common, which did not make me like her more.

Unlike most of us, who had transferred into the New School, Calvin had started at the New School and was transferring to Reed at the end of the semester. Ever since he'd made the decision to leave he was full of contempt for our school and our city, where he lived in what he told us was a great East Village railroad one-bedroom whose only drawback was that he had to share it with his ex-girlfriend. They had been "broken up," he said, for six months, but due to lease problems and space constraints they still slept in the same bed, which he said took up more than half their apartment's square footage. Unfortunately none of the resultant drama made it into his short stories, which were about the lives and problems of thirtysomething men with dangerous jobs and stunningly overactive sex lives. The stories were derivative of something, nothing you could put your finger on. They were a little bit derivative of everything, like a Norton short fiction anthology in a blender. The class liked these stories, not because they were good but because they were easy to have a discussion about: there were plots and characters and narrative structures and no one in them was obviously Calvin, so we didn't have to worry about hurting anyone's feelings, not that we ever really worried about that.

Calvin's characters were muscular and immaculately

groomed, given to feats of strength and endurance. Calvin himself was skinny and typically dressed in corduroys and Goodwill striped polo shirts, and he'd grown a weedy thatch of hair around his mouth and chin in order to seem older. His lips, in amongst the hair, were plump and girlishly red, perpetually chapped, probably because he was always nervously licking them.

Ellen was tough-looking in the Scarlett vein, although possibly not a lesbian. She had a wide, friendly face with squinty eyes and a mop of blond hair cut like Dennis the Menace's. Because she was from Massachusetts and her stories were often about drinking, I associated her pleasantly with Eileen Myles. Her stories seemed like they came to her effortlessly, and this made them good.

After the critique of Scarlett's story wrapped up, we reconnoitered on the sidewalk and then decided to head to the bar where we always went, on University. Once there we put our backpacks down on some couches and ordered drinks. Scarlett ordered for all of us: a round of double Jamesons on the rocks. The two-for-one happy hour special was ending soon, so there ended up being two drinks in front of each of us, two doubles. After these drinks, I reasoned, I would stop drinking and go home and get started on the long story that was due the following Monday, the one I had not yet started though we'd been assigned it since the beginning of the semester.

I'd be a little bit buzzed, probably, but it would help my ideas flow more freely.

Somehow a little while later we were walking east, to another bar, where the drinks were cheaper. Lana was drunk already but trying to act sober in a school-marmish way that she had. It is dickish, on the slim side-walks of East 7th Street, to walk more than two abreast, so our walking configuration had turned into: Ellen and Scarlett, me and Lana, and Calvin bringing up the rear. "I'm sorry I said that about your story," Lana told me. She could have been referring to anything she had ever said about any of my stories, but it didn't matter. My heart swelled with affection for Lana. I loved her wool skirt and her sensible flats. She began to resemble an illustration on a '60s Butterick pattern to me. She wob-bled down the sidewalk like a walking doll with a bro-ken mechanism. I of course saw myself as entirely sober, though writing a story had started to seem like a little bit less of a possibility.

It was red-lighted nighttime already inside the next bar. Swarms of hard-drinking adults surrounded the pool table, serious players who had been there since four. We found a little table to sit around but there wasn't enough room for all of us to sit, so I sat on Scarlett's lap. Calvin bought us all several rounds of bottled Bud-weisers. Eventually Scarlett started punching me in the arm. "You like that, don't you?" I punched her back, flattered that she was flirting with me even though it was painful. "You like it, you like it, say that you like it," she growled, punching me in the same spot over and over. We started wrestling around a little, and the feeling of being in a physical fight was exhilarating even though I was terrible at fighting. I instinctively grabbed for her hair but Scarlett, who had clearly been in a fight or two before, grabbed my arm, the one she'd been punching, and twisted it around behind my back. At this point I was squealing in an undignified way and it was starting to attract attention, and also we were on the floor. After smothering me for a hot moment in an Old Spicey choke hold, Scarlett let me get up. Calvin cleared his throat and suggested we all go outside and have a cigarette.

Scarlett and I were sweaty and red but Lana looked green. "I might go home, you guys, I'm running low on cash," she told us. "I am too," I said, though I hadn't paid for any drinks yet. Calvin suggested heading to his place a couple of blocks over, where there were some bottles of wine and his ex-girlfriend would probably not be home, or if she was home, she probably wouldn't mind the company.

When we got there we all realized how drunk we were in the way that you only can in the presence of someone who is doing something sober and productive. Calvin's ex-girlfriend, a neat brunette, was sitting at a desk that was stacked with books about South America, drinking water from a Nalgene bottle. She grimaced at Calvin and said something to him in a voice we couldn't hear, but then got up and started to rearrange furniture so that there would be someplace for us to sit besides their bed. It really did take up half the room.

The room was beautiful despite its tininess, with inset cabinets and high ceilings and lots of bookshelves and band posters on the walls. If its inhabitants hated each other, their psychic pain hadn't etched itself into the space. Maybe the space was just too old and resilient to be affected by turmoil in the lives of some college students who'd only been renting it for a couple of years.

They'd put lamps around the room, and amber filtered in through sheer blinds from the streetlamp outside, so the room felt warm. It was overall a nearly ideal place to be drunk.

Calvin got us all tumblers of wine and packed a bowl, and as we smoked it we talked about writers we admired and writing and What Is Art. As soon as she was high, Calvin's girlfriend became a welcome addition to the group; we could tell her stories about things that had happened earlier in the night and cement our group identity. I came back from a trip to the tiny bathroom and made a joke about the poster on the back of the bathroom door: "It's the Belle and SeBathroom!" Everyone fell out laughing; Scarlett's handsome face especially was contorted with helpless teary laughter. We weren't writ-

ers or waiters or editorial assistants then, not yet. We
were just in college.

The next day I was a waitress, a waitress with a hangover. If my waitressing jobs were plotted on a graph with
"lucrative" on the bottom axis and "exploitative" on the
side, this job was the furthest into the lower lefthand
corner I had ever been, a trade off I was willing to make
after years of jobs in the upper righthand corner (and
even a few in the hard-to-explain upper lefthand corner).
Hardly anyone besides a few cranky regulars ever sat
and ate at Hello? Café—most of the business came from
deliveries of the inexpensive generic American food to
apartments in nearby Stuy Town or nurses at the hospi-
tals further up Second Avenue. One woman called every
day to ask what the soup of the day was; I got the impression that I was one of only a few nonfeline beings
she interacted with on regular basis. Like many of our
patrons, she often ordered a bottle or two of wine for delivery with her dinner. My fellow staff members included
the owner and his son and his son's girlfriend, insanely
hardworking Chinese immigrants who were usually too
busy shouting at their army of insanely hardworking
Chinese cooks and delivery guys to concern themselves

much with what I was doing. What I was doing was usually either answering the phone or walking absently through the empty restaurant, pretending to wipe down the tables and thinking about what I would order for staff meal. All the owners seemed to care about was that I wore my uniform, a black tank top emblazoned with the café's question-mark logo.

But because it was Saturday there were actual patrons, lured by the café's cheap brunch specials. I served piles of hollandaise-coated eggs and grease-soaked potatoes and filled and refilled cups of coffee, occasionally taking breaks to go out to the backyard and sit with my head between my knees, trying not to puke.

At around two I felt that my condition had stabilized enough that I could swallow some Advil, and then after it kicked in I started almost enjoying myself. There is something quasi-voluptuous about a hangover when you're beginning to come out of it: the cozy feeling as the iron vise around your temples transforms into a cottony headband that's only slightly too tight. My limbs ached pleasantly, as though I'd worked out. I approached a table of middle-aged ladies who'd had a few moments with their menus and smiled and asked them what they'd like to order. The first lady kept squinting at her menu through her reading glasses as she ordered, but her friend made uninterrupted eye contact with me as she told me how she'd like her eggs cooked. "Fries or hash browns?"

I asked. "Hash browns, and, miss, can I tell you something, and please don't be offended?" she said. And then she pointed to the bruise on my arm.

There was no mirror in the bathroom where I changed into my uniform so I hadn't noticed that the spot where Scarlett had punched me repeatedly had, overnight, transformed into something so horrifying that it was difficult to look at. No wonder my tips had been higher than usual! The bruise was oblong, with an inner circle of rust-colored broken capillaries on a sunset-purple backdrop. There was really no accidental way that someone would be able to get such a bruise, and this woman knew it: "There's a place you can go," she said, "where he won't be able to find you." The look in her eyes was urgent and pained.

I didn't know how to explain what had happened. "I was play-fighting with this lesbian in my writing workshop and we got a little carried away." Nope. Instead I stammered out something about slipping and falling that must have sounded straight out of an Oxygen movie called something like *Denial*. She shook her head at me ruefully and then continued to steal sad glances at me the entire time she and her friend ate their eggs. I bustled around the restaurant, trying hard to project not-abusedness. The business card that they left with the tip got scraped, unexamined, into the trash on top of their toast crusts and plastic jam packages when I bussed their table.

That night, after work, I told Joseph what had happened and we stood in the bathroom and laughed, marveling at the bruise, which you could tell was destined to turn a rainbow of shades from deep plum to a final sickly chartreuse on its way back to just being skin. But after he fell asleep I lay there next to him on his futon and stared up at the ceiling and remembered that a boy *had* hit me once, though it had been unclear, then, which of us had been abusing the other.

Kenyon was a strange place to be a girl—it just was; this was one of the first things I learned about it. When I finally visited the campus during senior year of high school, after having been accepted there and pretty much nowhere else, and the girl who I stayed with during my visit told me that she had been raped by another student the semester prior, it was too late to cross Kenyon off my list. She was casual about telling me: "Here's Gund Dining Hall. Here's the student center. Near here I was raped." I wanted to believe that it was one of those cases of drunken confusion or retracted consent. I was trying to have a good time on my visit.

I filed the information away alongside my impression of the dining hall food. There were two waiting lists I was still waiting to hear about. By the time I realized I would have to attend Kenyon, the details of my visit had blurred—I had visited a lot of other schools, too, after all—and all I could remember from my visit was the dimness of the girl's dorm, a riot-proof structure from the '70s with slit windows that didn't open, so the smell of musty carpet and mildew was trapped inside forever.

When I say I went to school in Ohio, people usually assume I went to Oberlin, that breeding ground of cool bands and Ultimate Frisbee championships and general Williamsburg, Brooklyn training camp some miles to Kenyon's north, and even after I say I went to Kenyon I think people are sometimes still imagining Oberlin. Aside from the fact that it was in Ohio, Kenyon was nothing like Oberlin. Kenyon may be the anti-Oberlin. Its dress code was preppy and its intellectual climate was second-rate conservatism. It was a place for people who'd flunked out of several elite East Coast boarding schools, who'd been denied admission at Yale despite being double legacies. It was a summer camp for the loser younger brothers of the ruling class, and its social life was entirely dependent, you learned immediately—like on your first night there, hours after your parents finished helping move you in—on frat parties. Some were held in the woods at frat lodges and others held in the historic dorms on the south quad where the elder frat boys were granted blocks by the housing lottery. Strangely, there were no sororities, supposedly because of how recently (1969) the school had gone coed. The frat brothers picked the freshmen girls they'd invite to their parties by circling the pictures they liked in the freshman "facebook," which in 1999 was a tangible object, a little booklet circulated by the school's administration. I saw a marked-up facebook once: blue circles for "pretty," check marks for "maybe," yellow *x* for "definitely don't invite her."

Status came from being a frat boy's girlfriend, and I was interested in status. Also it was becoming clear that Kenyon wasn't a good place to be single. During my first weeks there I'd pursued what seemed like a loose, funny flirtation at one of these frat parties, ending up in a classically handsome Delta Kappa Epsilon's dorm room where, he said, we would watch *Goodfellas*. I wasn't naive enough to think that we were really there to watch a movie, but I *was* naive enough to think that we would just make out first-dateishly. When I balked at the steady pressure of his hand on the back of my head, he calmly explained that there was no reason for me not to suck his dick because even if I didn't he'd still say that I had, which he did.

He called me a bitch as I got up to leave and told me I would not find any more invitations to DKE parties in my student mailbox, which turned out to be true. I heard about this guy later on that he celebrated his twenty-first birthday by flying every single one of his fellow DKEs to Vegas and giving them each either $1,000 or $5,000 in chips to get them started (reports varied). More recently, his name caught my eye as I read an article about the bankruptcy of Lehman Brothers.

I don't remember how I met the boy who would become my frat-boy boyfriend but I remember him telling me how he first noticed me: during a ritual in the first week of school where all the freshmen had to parade down the college's "middle path," ending up on the steps of the colonnaded auditorium where they would stand again, four years later, to receive their diplomas. The upperclassmen booed and jeered as the freshmen sang a traditional hymn to their alma mater, a song that rhymed "asphodel" and "fare-thee-well" and prominently mentioned the river that flows by the campus. "I saw you in that short skirt and I was like, Who is that girl?"

Max was a Psi Upsilon, two years older than I was, a junior. He loved to drink and smoke weed, and he was from the Pacific Northwest so he was snobby about the haylike, headachy marijuana Ohio farmers planted in amongst their corn. He would only condescend to smoke it during the rare dry spells between his shipments, which were sent to him from his hometown in plastic bags submerged in family-size jars of Skippy. He sold the sticky, peanut-buttery-smelling nuggets to everyone from his fellow Psi Us to the dining hall employees. We would smoke these until it began to seem like a good idea to heat up the deep fryer in the kitchen that itself had been a late-night whim, purchased over the phone from an infomercial's call center. We deep-fried everything available, from tomatoes to fun-size candy bars to pieces of old stale dining hall bread.

Max had a cute snaggly incisor on the left side of his full mouth and a compact, hairless body. His body was the first one I ever got to know very well, and I knew it much better than I ever got to know his brain, even though for a year we slept in the same bed almost every night. Sometimes I would come back to his dorm room during a fifteen-minute break between morning classes for a few minutes of frantic sex. In this realm we were both determined to the point of compulsivity. I remember all the locations where, because we both had roommates, and because we didn't live in a real town, we routinely fucked: the bathroom of the radio station, a clearing in the woods, the basement of the Psi Upsilon lodge. What I don't remember, besides the short-skirt comment and a few other sexual compliments, was a single conversation we ever had. I was too much of a romantic to articulate this to myself at the time, but I think that even then I understood what we were doing. We had made a bargain that involved saying "I love you" because that was what people did in these situations, but what we actually loved was the license to treat each other's bodies like complex bionic sex toys. If we'd really loved each other we probably wouldn't have been able to sustain what we were doing physically; we would have respected each other too much to keep doing that to each other. It felt good and damaging in equal measure, the same way getting drunk and high every day feels, and obviously we were doing those things too.

Drinking is a skill. Max was just not very good at it, and experience wasn't making him better. He would get red-faced and sloppy and start slurring his words after about four beers, and he would go on to drink six or seven more. Midway through my sophomore year I started to get bored of this. I was spending more time hanging out with the rich hippies of the campus, a contingent of jam-band-listening kids I'd met in the art barn who liked to get high and listen to music or watch *Annie Hall*, not football. The logical thing to do would have been to break up with Max, but I was too addicted to the various stimulations that our relationship reliably provided. So instead I embarked on a secret parallel life, insofar as that's possible in a town with fewer than two thousand inhabitants. The centerpiece of my secret life was a crush on a boy in my drama class, a long-haired lothario who bore a slight resemblance, mostly just jaw-wise, to a young Mick Jagger. Eventually I succeeded in having sex with him, or something like sex—we had smoked opium, so whatever we did was done in a blurry and half-asleep state that made details hard to remember afterward.

One afternoon I woke up from a nap in Max's bed to find him standing over me, holding a notebook where I'd written—I shudder to think how badly—about my addled encounter with the drama-class hippie. This was surreal in and of itself, like one of those nightmares where you "wake up" and are still in the nightmare. He was shouting at me to get out, that I was a bitch, a slut, et cetera, and I was trying to feel guilty and remorseful— in theory, you know, we cared about each other—but I was so sleepy. I wished he would just let me go back to sleep for five more minutes and even thought about asking him whether this was an option; I was probably hungover. Soon, though, I was fully awake and staring in disbelief as Max grabbed armfuls of my things, everything I'd left in his room—pieces of my Halloween costume, coats and sweaters and boots—and took them out to his front yard, where he hurled them onto the grass in a sloppy pile. This seemed a bit excessive, but I understood his position. I grabbed what I could—I got the notebook, at least—and ran back to my dorm room. I thought I would let him cool down for a bit. Later that night—I don't quite remember how I spent the intervening hours, probably talking to whoever would listen and definitely drinking, because I got melodramatically drunk—I remembered that the Psi U's were having a party that night, and I decided to go apologize to Max.

I wandered alone over to the party at the lodge, and

when Max saw me he immediately dragged me outside, to the flagstone path leading up to the lodge's front door. I could have turned and left then, but I wasn't reacting very quickly. I should have just run away—well, clearly I should never have come—but instead I was crying, un-dignified, babbling frantically, talking about love. Max was crying too; his face was red and wet and his voice was breaking like a teenager's. He wasn't that much big-ger than me, but he was heavier and stronger.

There had always been something like violence in the driven insistence between us, but this time it wasn't tem-pered by anything like tenderness. After he pushed me down and I slipped and hit my head on the flagstones, I had thought he was trying to help me up. But the guy who came and intervened must have realized earlier than I did what Max was really doing, which was lifting me up by the shoulders so that he could slam me down again. He pulled Max off me before my head could hit the flagstones a second time.

It was too late to write about this for memoir class so I put some frills around the story, including setting it a bit earlier in the school year so that the party would fall on Halloween, and making the rescuer at the end be dressed up as Jesus on the cross (which someone had really done one Halloween at Kenyon), and in this way I turned it into "fiction." I made photocopies and handed them out to Dot, to Scarlett, to Calvin, to Ellen, and to Lana.

During critique, Lana raised her hand first, as usual. She wanted to know why the narrator character had written about her infidelity in a diary, why the diary was in a place where her boyfriend could find it. "That's just the kind of thing she does," I said.

5

What Needs to Be Done

My first nine-to-five job really did start at nine; if I got there any later than nine ten there was a chance—slim, because he usually didn't arrive until ten, but a chance still—that I wouldn't be at my desk before Jim got to his, and it was humiliating to dash down the hall to my cubicle to see that he'd unlocked his own office door and was sitting inside, his turned back bristling with mild irritation even as he greeted me cheerfully. If I had a couple of late days in a row he would remind me, with a condescending gentleness that was worse than anger, that it was my job to open his door, sort his mail and newspapers, and take anything he'd put in his outbox back to my desk to circulate or sort or file or rewrite before he got to his desk. He wanted to arrive at the office to checked messages and sorted papers, a veneer of organization overlaying the chaos. This ritualized servility and all its officey accoutrements—the coffee, the dry-cleaned outfits, the comfortable low-heeled pumps—thrilled me with their adult feel. On my first day Jim had ceremoniously presented me with a book he said he gave to all new employees, a slim paperback titled *Don't Just Do What I Tell You to Do, Do What Needs to Be Done*. He'd been its editor; he'd edited many of the management-technique best sellers put out by the publishing house where we both worked, he as editor in chief and I as his editorial assistant. I read the whole book that night, and for the next three years I did my best—I really did—not just to do what I was told to do but to do what needed to be done, for Jim but also eventually for myself.

One surprise was that my duties included making little jokes all day, subtly colluding with Jim against whoever was peeving him at any given moment. I would give my voice the slightest mocking intonation or just roll my eyes while delivering a stack of phone message slips all bearing the name of the same pestering literary agent or needy editor. This wasn't an onerous responsibility at all; Jim's veneer of inviolable diplomacy concealed a hilarious vein of petty bitchiness, and while he deplored this

weakness in himself—he was a good person and a skill-
ful boss, always striving to be fair—it was my favorite
thing about him. He was generally so circumspect and
straitlaced that when he did let a bit of gossip slip, about
an author who'd run through an advance too quickly
or an agent who'd cheated on his wife, I felt an unprecedented glow. I had never felt so clever in anyone's presence as I did in his.

In college I'd had a half-acknowledged fantasy that a
teacher would recognize some talent in me and decide to
make me her protégé, but it had never happened, probably because I was such a prickly and pretentious little
jerk, with no innate gift for ass-kissing. Jim didn't want
his ass kissed. He seemed, oddly enough, to want me to
tell the truth, especially if that meant saying the obnoxious things he was too couth to admit he thought, too.

The closest analog to my relationship with Jim thus
far in my life was my relationship with Phillip, whose
bitchy streak was somewhat less well-concealed but who
also made me feel brilliant—we both felt brilliant whenever we talked to each other. A few months earlier he'd
moved into the apartment I'd just started sharing with
Joseph so that we could talk all the time (and so I could
pay less rent, and so it would seem less momentous that I
had moved in with my boyfriend). Phillip had even indi-
rectly gotten me the interview with Jim: some publishing
higher-up Phillip had been sleeping with had mentioned

that Jim was looking for an assistant. It was a more administrative position than I'd been looking for, but I'd
been looking, at that point, for three months, and temp-
ing intermittently and running though my graduation-
gift money at a truly alarming rate. Very few potential
employers besides Jim had even had me in for an interview, so I sat down on his office couch scarily under-
rehearsed and proceeded, I thought, to ruin my chances.

Jim asked me what the last movie I'd seen was and
I'd told him it was the Bertolucci movie *The Dreamers*,
which is about French teenagers having sex in 1969. "Did
you like it?" he asked. I told him that I'd been told it
was "like porn," and had therefore been disappointed: it
had turned out to be like extraordinarily boring, densely
plotted porn. Jim half-laughed with a look of shock in
his eyes and I nervously adjusted my skirt, which was not
only too short but was also covered in cat hair. The hairs
had been invisible in my dim apartment, but in the fluo-
rescent office overheads they positively glistened. It took
all my self-restraint not to start nervously plucking them
off while Jim asked me questions about my résumé. I had
gone to school for writing and so, he wondered, did I
want to be a writer? Recognizing this as a trick question,
I talked about how much I'd enjoyed marking up my
classmates' stories in workshop classes—this, I said, was
where I felt my true talent lay. "Good," he said. "Writers
make terrible editorial assistants. Rick Moody—terrible

editorial assistant." I nodded as though I were personally familiar with Rick Moody's shoddy filing skills.

Lucky for me, and for my parents with whom I would have had to move in with if my unemployment had lasted more than another couple of weeks, and for Phillip and Joseph who would have been forced to find a new room-mate, Jim recognized my potential through the scrim of cat hair. I started work the following week.

Phillip had moved in a few months prior, around New Year's, when I'd finished the last of my course require-ments at the New School. Joseph was the only member of our household who had a job then, and Phillip and I would wake as he was leaving for it, around eleven, and then busy ourselves with the task of wasting the rest of the day. If my temp agency hadn't called me in—they hardly ever did—I would sit at my computer in the unwin-dowed middle "office" room of our railroad apartment in the upper reaches of Nassau Avenue in Greenpoint, looking at job listings online. I searched the job descrip-tions, looking for a position that seemed to have what I was looking for, but I couldn't find one. It would have helped, I guess, if I'd any idea what I was looking for. It wasn't because I'd never thought about this before I'd graduated—on the contrary, the question of my career had obsessed me, and I'd done five unpaid internships, testing the waters of different traditional English-majory realms of endeavor—but the only conclusion I'd drawn was that I didn't want to work at any of the places I'd interned.

Those three months were the laziest of my life. After I would finish up my morning—really midafternoon—job-searching, Phillip and I would sometimes muster our energies and leave the house. We'd walk, or take the bus if the weather was too cold and bleak, to cafés in main-drag Williamsburg where we would sit the same way we did at our kitchen table at home, drinking coffee and talking aimlessly. We would talk about the future while holding it forcibly at bay with our inactivity. We drank hundreds of cups of coffee—my graduation money was trickling, or really gushing, away in frothy puddles of latte—and hatched thousands of schemes, of which only a couple ever came to fruition.

We felt the burden of our unemployment as a squandered opportunity, but we weren't brave enough or rich enough to do anything interesting with our spare time. We thought we should be writing novels, or volunteering. We knew that the animal shelter in Williamsburg was always looking for people to walk its dogs, and so we put our names on the roster of volunteer dog-walkers there. The idea was that we would from then on spend our days traipsing down the fashionable streets together with purpose, occasionally striking up conversations with other dog owners as our adorable charges sniffed each others' butts. Owning a dog or even just being mistaken for someone who owned a dog seemed like an important announcement of belonging, a declaration of the long-term intent to stay in New York and a badge of adulthood and responsibility. Anyone who saw you with your temporary dog would assume that you lived in an apartment, the nicer kind that allowed pets, and that not only could you afford the rent there but you could also pay for dog food and veterinary care. We aspired to all these things and were thrilled that someone would allow us to credibly pretend to have them, even just for an hour.

When we showed up for our first session, though, I was unceremoniously handed the leash of a mangy terrier who, I was told, had problems with men—I should cross the street if I saw any because she couldn't be trusted not to attack them. Also, socializing with other dogs was not allowed under any circumstances. Phillip and I were therefore nonnegotiably forced to walk in opposite directions. He strolled away in the direction of the trash-strewn waterfront park at North 3rd Street with his elderly, slow-moving miniature poodle, a sad white creature with patches of taupe-stained fur around its mouth and rear. Meanwhile, the terrier dragged me down various deserted industrial side streets where we were battered by the icy winds whipping off the East River. It was unusually cold that winter. Our escape from our depressing apartment was turning out to also be depressing, and cold.

After I started my job, Phillip and I quickly developed a new routine. He still stayed up all night writing and going to the Metropolitan gay bar and doing nothing, so that when I got up for work I'd catch him just before he finally went to sleep. During this overlap in our waking hours, we would sit in our living room and blearily watch the soothing, banal first hour of the *Today* show together. The incipient appearances of the authors and "authors" my employer published would be trumpeted, and I'd feel a part of something large and important. Also, Katie Couric, then in her penultimate year of hosting the show, would sometimes remind me of myself: fundamentally unhappy to be up so early but determined to power through by pretending to a kind of droll, ultra-professional chipperness. Phillip and I agreed that one day we'd get up—well, I'd get up—extra early and go to Rockefeller Center to stand in the throng of well-wishers outside the studio, holding up signs, maybe wearing face paint. We never did this, either.

I began my job full of the thrilling sense of life being lived to the utmost. Every moment, I felt I was learning something new about how the world worked. As Jim's authors and their agents called, I introduced myself, telling all the authors—as Jim had suggested—that I was a big fan of their books. ("Authors are vain," he'd explained when I'd balked at the lie. "No one is ever going to ask you, 'Okay, what's on page 203?'" He was right, of course.) I could almost feel the new neural pathways—ones having to do with patience and smooth sociability—forming in my brain. On my second day, Jim stepped out of his office and told me very tactfully that I was answering the phone in an overly fake tone of voice, and that I should just be myself. This was true: I'd affected a performative receptionisty chirp. I got rid of it quickly; certainly I had plenty of opportunity to practice, since the phone rarely stopped ringing. Some authors seemed just to want someone to talk to, to reassure themselves, as they sat at home toiling at their solitary tasks, that someone still cared what they were up to. I wanted to tell them to just start Googling themselves, but instead I humored them as best I could. "Where is that old rascal?" they'd ask, a begging note mixed into their jocularity. "Every time I call he's in a meeting. You all must have meetings about what the next meeting will be about!" I was generous with my laughter. It was so easy to make people like me in this context. It had never been easier, really. As they waited for Jim outside his office, the senior editors confided in and complained to me, and I could sense them trying to win me over. I had a kind of unearned, refracted power because I controlled access to their boss; it was in their best interest to have me on their side. I felt accepted into these smart, verbal, hypercritical people's ranks, finally somehow at home.

But as summer arrived and failed to bring with it, for

the first time in my life, the promise of a three-month break, the things I'd first found thrillingly adult about my job—the formal outfits, the ritualistic trips at appointed hours to the cafeteria for oatmeal and toast and coffee, the everyday humoring of old-school assholes who'd call me "sweetie" when I showed them into Jim's office and after I brought them coffee—began to grate on me. Keeping pace with Jim, who maintained a brisk roster of business breakfasts, lunches, and dinners and regularly spent entire weekend days at the office, filling his out-box until its topmost layers teetered precariously in the air-conditioning's canned breeze, required constant vigilance. He had to sign off on every tiny decision anyone in the editorial department made, in addition to actually editing his authors' books, and it was my job to be aware of every tiny decision that needed to be made, and whether it had been made yet, and if not, when it would be.

I would get home late, frayed from my three-train-plus-bus commute from the Upper West Side to Nassau Avenue, and smelly because I'd skipped a morning shower in favor of a few extra moments of sleep, and find Phillip and Joseph sitting at the kitchen table in their boxers, pursuing their passions. Joseph was programming computer music and Phillip was pecking away at his book. As a child, I'd been mystified when my dad would come home at nine and not want to play with me—he'd rushed, instead, to reheat and eat the leftovers from dinner, and then to lie on the couch downstairs watching golf highlights in a silent daze until he fell asleep. Sometimes I would sit with him, absorbing nothing of the game but happy just to be there beside him. Now, I understood.

I'd had some vague idea that, contrary to what I'd told Jim, I'd be a good editorial assistant—much better than Rick Moody, certainly—and also manage, in my spare time, to become a writer. Now as I sat in the weekly editorial meeting as we reviewed proposals for new books about trends and celebrities and memoirs by trendy celebrities, and talked more generally about what trends and celebrities had filtered into our consciousness—"Oh, I *love* her," was something you heard a lot, around that table—I was realizing that the production of book-shaped products had very little to do with "books," the holy relics that my college education had been devoted to venerating. I mean, I had known this before but now I knew the details of it, and also I was complicit in the making of these products.

I thought that I wanted to be like the other women in these meetings, the editors with their air of put-upon importance and their beautiful office clothes. They had immaculate makeup and gleaming, tasteful wedding bands. They had children; some were their families' breadwinners. The other assistants were sweaty, paper cut–scarred, but fiery-eyed; like me, they wanted what these women had: lunch meetings at Nougatine with Brooke Shields and a manicure that never chipped and sweet, unposed photos of beautiful children on their desks between the organized piles.

But in order to advance from editorial assistant to assistant editor, and from there to associate editor, I would have to champion specific products—I would have to take a proposal to the "acqs" meeting and convince the sales manager, the marketing manager, the publicity manager, the president, the publisher, and Jim that we would be able to transform the proposal into a worthy product. I felt silly for feeling shocked by the quality of what made it through. I knew it was immature to cling to beliefs like, for example, that books should be written by the person whose name was on the cover. I talked to Jim about these feelings a little bit, in a jokey way, and he reminded me that sometimes we had the opportunity to publish great books and that these unprofitable books were paid for by the celebrity memoirs. He had been in the business for twenty years and had earned the right to publish a few pet "real" authors—a gay author, a Chinese author—whose glowingly reviewed books only sold a few thousand copies. But he had to earn that right anew every season with a roster of pop-Zen doorstops, business-management guides, and cookbooks.

One morning during my third month of work, I sat

down at my desk and was overcome with some kind of sudden-onset stomach flu. I told my closest office friend how I was feeling and he told me to just go home, which hadn't occurred to me—I hadn't missed a day of work yet, and I hadn't planned ever to. I sat at my desk for another few minutes feeling feverish and nauseated, terrified that someone would come by with some task that would require me to interact or move. Eventually I left a note for Jim, who was in a meeting, and dashed out of the building. Once I was on the subway headed home, though, my lightheaded nausea faded and my racing pulse slowed. As an experiment I got off the train and waited in the tunnel until another one came headed in the opposite direction, back toward the office. As it roared into the station my stomach clenched and flipped, and I scanned the platform for the nearest trash can in case I vomited. But as the train left without me on it, I started feeling better again.

Panic attacks and constant gnawing pain in my stomach quickly became as routine to me as my commute and my morning coffee. I started seeing a therapist, who advised me to cut out the coffee, led me through breathing exercises, and diagnosed me with an anxiety disorder. I informed Jim of this diagnosis in hushed tones, the same way we spoke about a celebrity in editorial meeting when a *People* magazine article revealed that she had cancer. ("Do we know what kind of cancer? Should I write a letter to her agent? Too soon?") He didn't seem too concerned, and this was the perfect response—had he furrowed his brow and treated me like an invalid, I would've felt his loss of confidence in me as a devastating insult. He knew I'd be able to do an excellent job no matter what, he told me.

I didn't take a vacation that summer but I did get to relax a bit. The volume of calls and submissions slackened substantially as the agents and authors fled the city, leaving us their phone numbers in Nantucket and Martha's Vineyard and the Hamptons to be called in case of dire emergency. The higher-up editors took more "editing at home" days and even we assistants were granted half-day Fridays. Jim remained at his desk, though, so I did too, but with less to do, I spent more time scouting the Internet for new literary talent. I started spending several hours a day reading a site called Gawker, which, because it was devoted to "Manhattan media gossip," could be construed as having some work-related relevance. I quickly got to the point where I would sit down at my desk and the first letter my fingers would automatically type would be *G,* which would autofill the URL bar of my browser with Gawker.com. Gawker introduced me to other blogs, but mostly it introduced me to itself. And I thought something along the lines of, That looks like fun.

So Phillip and I started a blog. It was called The Universal Review and its mission was to review everything in the universe and assign it letter grades, most of which were quite low. I contributed reviews of quotidian office experiences, like elevator chat ("I love those shoes") and random discarded meeting-food scavenged from the break room. Phillip reviewed "being a writer" (not all it was cracked up to be, apparently, though from where I was sitting, from the cubicle where I was sitting, it seemed just fine) and "walking other people's dogs" and "being a slut," which at that time were his main areas of expertise. Heartbreak was another: his first love had dumped him rather mercilessly, and everything he wrote was tinged by this, even when it was hilarious, and this lent our blog an air of gravitas. For my part, I was lighthearted, mostly, with only slight hints of sadness: reviewing the bums who hung out on the corner on our new block in a slightly more accessible part of Greenpoint. I said that when I passed them on my way to the subway in the morning, I was sometimes struck by a pang of envy (I gave them a D anyway). And I reviewed "brain drugs," writing about losing the ability to judge anything accurately due to the numbing effects of Zoloft, which made all of my experiences seem to deserve the same bland C+.

In the spring of that year I went to a party where I ran into a lot of people from Kenyon. The party reminded me of the experiences that had catalyzed my decision to leave after sophomore year, and I wrote a C+ review of Kenyon—its sexist frat culture and the Ivy-reject boarding school kids who took part in it—on The Universal Review.

The next day there was a scathing comment posted on the site. It was clearly from someone who'd known me at Kenyon, but the commenter didn't leave a name or any identifying details, just a solid paragraph about how I was narcissistic, immature, unliked, and untalented. Phillip and I joked about the comment and debated deleting it, but I decided to approve it and then responded with a comment of my own (no one should ever do this) pointing out the cowardice of the commenter's anonymity. Then I resolved to put it out of my mind. Then I checked several times a day for the next few weeks to see whether the commenter had responded.

Three summers later I had become an associate editor with my own small office, though I was still Jim's assistant—neither of us felt ready to give the other up completely yet, and I was allowed to assign some of the administrative parts of the job to an editorial assistant. And I had my own blog, begun after Phillip and I had dissolved our partnership after one of the cutthroat spats that had marked the inevitable end of our time as roommates. One of Gawker's longtime editors had just announced that she was leaving and, reading the announcement, I entertained a fantasy of replacing her that seemed hilariously far-fetched, from where I sat.

Where I sat, that week, was the dark, masculine office of the president of my company, trying not to stare rudely at the people sitting on his couch. They were the stars of a then–hugely popular reality show about bounty hunters and they had deep, leathery tans and a powerful smell of cologne and cigarette smoke. They were there to try to close a very nice deal for the bounty hunter's memoirs, which had at one point been promised to another publisher. There had been a falling-out with that house, though, some problem with the ghostwriter—the bounty hunter's wife, clearly the power behind the bounty-hunting throne, had disapproved of his methods and of the details of the bounty hunter's pre-marriage life he'd chosen to include. So they had come to my employer because this was the kind of book we published all the time. For some reason—maybe in the editorial meeting I'd said, "Oh, I *love* him," or maybe my bosses thought that my tattoos, visible that day in a short-sleeved blouse, would make the bounty hunter feel that he was among friends— I was going to be the "editor" of the book if we acquired it, though of course the deal required so much synergy and high-level strategy that it would be orchestrated by people with much more actual power. I would be in charge of the low-level headaches associated with the project—the inevitable barrages of worried phone calls, the houndings for payment by various subcontractors. I smiled at the bounty hunter and his wife and asked polite questions about how they were enjoying New York so far. The president and I assured them that we cared a lot about how the bounty hunter's story be told—the necessity of getting the truth out there. Really, everyone involved would have been happier if the deal had simply involved the exchange of suitcases of cash. The views from the president's office were spectacular. You could even see a little corner of Central Park, if you stood in exactly the right place.

I was spared having to deal with the bounty hunter book, though, because I got the job at Gawker. A friend who I knew through my blog recommended me and I interviewed and I auditioned and all the while I pretended not to know that I would get the job. But during the weekend of the audition—I stayed inside and wrote dozens of posts each day, mimicking the cutting voice I'd read so much of over the years that I'd spent bored at my desk—I had felt the thrill of virtuosity. Being mean and quick came easily to me, and if I thought about it, I could imagine that everything I'd done up until that point had been my training for this job. The hyperawareness of celebrity culture I'd developed at the publishing house served me well, certainly, but I was also reminded—as I sat there during the audition, barely rising from my desk to pee or eat pieces of toast—of my high-school-era proclivity for frantic, constant note-passing. I had even maintained a notebook solely for the purpose of writing nasty little observations about my teachers and classmates, which my friends and I would circulate to each other in class. At one point it had been confiscated and a teacher we'd been particularly cruel to had punished us; I had protested the punishment, citing the first amendment rights we'd been studying that semester in Government class.

A few days before I officially found out that I had the job, I found myself at a party at Gawker's millionaire owner's loft in SoHo. I came with a bottle of champagne; I put it in the kitchen, along with all the other bottles of champagne. The loft was full of hard-edged furniture and it had high, high ceilings. There weren't so many people there, but I knew most of them; I'd met them by taking them out to lunch during my years of finding new literary talent online. They smiled at me; I poured myself a glass of the champagne I'd brought and took it over to the window where I stood, not even feeling awkward standing by myself. I could stand by myself at a party. I could decide who I wanted to talk to and when. I had made it this far; it felt like I'd scaled something. In a way I had, and in a way I was at the bottom. But I would climb, and fall, and climb.

6

Off-Leash

Lee is the first thing I notice when I wake up in the morning, a heavy warmth in the bed next to me, almost like a person. Since I've been sleeping next to a person for the last few years, her presence isn't uncomfortable, except at the moment when I realize she is a dog, not a person. Then it's like I'm feeling around for the place where pain will be—poking at a blister and finding that the stretched skin is a little bit sore but mostly just tautly menacing, full of the threat of popping.

Lee observes the change in my breathing and immediately gets that I'm awake and starts barking and whining and wagging her tail, begging to be taken to the park. She is a beautiful, endearingly stupid pit bull mix with a brown spot on her yellow back that's like a button you can press to make her happy. She likes to have the spot gently thumped. I roll out of bed and thump her for a while and then I get dressed. It's summer, so I don't have to do much in the way of getting dressed: flip-flops, gym shorts, ponytail. I feel butch and athletic. It's crazy to think that a few months ago I felt so weak and tired. A few months ago, I had sat on the edge of my bed on weekends, when there was no real reason to get out of bed, and cried, feeling the weakness radiating from the center of my chest all along my limbs. "Is it me? Do you think it's me?" Joseph had asked me. Later, he told me that this had been my chance to break up with him the right way, the clean, good way: "I asked!"

In the next room, my mom is asleep on the foldout couch. I invited her to the apartment where I'm dog-sitting while I wait to move into a new apartment—an apartment where, for the first time, I'll live alone. My friend Daria lives nominally alone in this apartment with Lee, but a tie rack in the closet is a sign that the arrangement isn't going to last much longer: Daria's boyfriend will move in, it's only a matter of time. Every girl lives with her boyfriend in New York; all of my friends do, at least, because living with your boyfriend means paying hundreds of dollars less per month in rent than you otherwise would. Sharing a one-bedroom is hundreds of dollars a month less expensive than living with a roommate and up to a thousand dollars a month less expensive than living alone, and in a city where a decently livable one-bedroom in anything like an okay neighborhood rents for a minimum of $1,600, you don't have to be a cheapskate or a cynic to make this calculation. This calculation makes it seem like it's a good idea to always be in love, or at least looking for love, or pretending to be looking or pretending to be in love.

For a minute, as I stand in the kitchen drinking a glass of orange juice from Daria's fridge, I let the future unspool in front of me a little bit. I think about how at some point I will want to just sit on the couch and watch TV on a Friday or Saturday night and how all of the people I'd want to do that with will be sitting on their own couches with their boyfriends. Maybe I'll invite myself over to sit with them and the boyfriends, all watching TV together. Maybe after the TV-watching I'll invite myself to crawl into bed between them, not for sex, I mean not exactly, just for the warm animal comfort of lying in bed with someone, talking idly about whatever before falling asleep.

Maybe I should get a dog.

My mom is yawning and stretching. "Good morning. Going to the park? Did you sleep well? This foldout couch is more comfortable than I thought it would be. Should I make some coffee, or finish the dishes from last night? I had a couple of strange dreams! You're up early!"

The nice thing about my mom being around is that it means I'm not alone. Not being alone keeps the blister unpopped. But then there's every other thing about my mom being around.

"I believe in observing at least a two-hour moratorium on speaking immediately after waking up," I try.

"Mmhm. Did you want to go to the bookstore today? You'd mentioned something about that. We have the rental car, so this is a good time to run errands! I need to eat something soon for my blood sugar." My mom is bustling around as she talks, folding the couch back up, running a comb through her pretty, sensibly bobbed hair. "I really did enjoy sleeping on this foldout couch! But I thought, in case we wanted to sit on it, I should fold it up. You might want to think about getting something like this for your new apartment. I think they're not too expensive." My mom's shoes are on now. There is nothing I can do to stop her from coming along to the park, and Lee is barking, circling around the door.

The summer that my parents were twenty-six, they got married. In the snapshots from their wedding, they're beautiful despite, or maybe because of, their 1977 haircuts and outfits. In an era before wedding-themed reality shows and bridal expos and "wedding photojournalists," my parents had stared into each others' eyes and promised to love only each other for the rest of their lives. Implicit in this promise were a series of subpromises: promises to move into an apartment and cook healthy meals together and snap more snapshots and have mutual friends and take beach vacations and have a baby and move into a town-house development and have another baby and move into a real house and work every day and send their children to college and have spats and take ballroom dancing classes and have complicated shared retirement plans.

This summer I am twenty-six and I am living temporarily in the windowless, unventilated attic of a loft in a converted warehouse whose inhabitants call it "the Beast House," with all my possessions—basically, a computer and some clothes—stuffed in garbage bags on the floor of my room.

When we get back from walking Lee, it's time to go to my old apartment to feed my and Joseph's cats, who weren't allowed to move to the already cat-replete Beast

House with me and anyway the custody details haven't been worked out yet. I assume we'll end up splitting the cats—there are two, so, perfect—but I'm not sure because I haven't talked to Joseph since I left. I haven't been back to the apartment, which he's now sharing with one of his bandmates, either. His band is playing a show in Boston this weekend, which is why neither he nor the roommate is available to feed the cats.

"What a beautiful day!" says my mom as, behind the wheel of the rental car, she straps on her dorky sunglasses. "Do you want a calcium softchew?" I shake my head. We drive under the BQE and through the Hasidic part of Williamsburg, with my mom talking the entire time about the scenery we're passing and what kind of people live in what neighborhood and the smell of steak blowing out of the exhaust vents at Peter Luger. She asks a lot of questions, like: Why is that building boarded up? Who would want to live in a fancy glass high-rise next door to a building that's boarded up? Which direction should she go on Division Street? I don't have any answers for her. I'm thinking of what the apartment might be like when I get there, and about the last time I'd been in it with Joseph.

It had been a Friday. The previous weekend, Joseph and I had gone to his family's house in Nantucket to give ourselves a last chance to salvage things after I had confessed to kissing someone else. The relationship-saving weekend had been strange and, like our initial confrontation about the cheating, full of terrible insults and weepy declarations that sounded like bad TV dialogue. "I wouldn't have told you if I didn't still want to be with you!" I said, and also, "It'll never happen again."

During the week between the relationship-saving weekend and that final Friday, I had continued to kiss someone else, and that afternoon this guy and I had walked through the Union Square Greenmarket and he had bought me a bottle of apple juice which we'd shared, kissing. I had then taken the subway all the way home to Greenpoint and I had gone to the C-Town and bought a Styrofoam package of lamb chops and a rubber-banded bunch of asparagus and a half-pint of heavy cream and angel hair pasta—a nice dinner, all the things Joseph liked, and I had come home and put the bag of groceries down in the kitchen and then I had gone to the living room to sit on the couch and stare into space, paralyzed. Finally Joseph came home. He sat down next to me on the couch and we looked straight into each other's eyes and, as a result of six years of practice, understood what was going on in each other's minds, mostly.

"It's over, isn't it," he said, not even bothering to end the sentence with a question mark, and then, yeah, it was.

A month later, here I am at the door of our old building, which is now just Joseph's building. My body still knows exactly how to twist the key, exactly how much weight to throw toward the door. At the curb, my mom sits in the rented SUV, double-parked, talking animatedly on her hands-free cell phone in a way that makes her look vaguely psycho. I turn back around and walk through the yellow vestibule, smelling the familiar kitcheny smells of the building. I'm numb. When I open the door of the apartment, though, the cats rush to greet me and automatic tears come to my eyes. They seem so happy to see me, even though I smell like dog, even though I've left them behind. I kneel to pet them and ask for their forgiveness and tell them how much I love them. The cats forgive me and understand what I'm feeling and they want to comfort me. Or they want food.

The biggest change in the apartment is that it smells like ass now. There are ashtrays overflowing with the crushed butts of American Spirits on every surface, and William has switched to the cheapest brand of kitty litter, the kind that gives small, exhaust fan–less New York apartments their special sad clay smell. The top note in the ass bouquet emanates from the room that looks out on the air shaft, which had been William's studio before. Now it's his bedroom, and it smells like his unique brand of pencil-shavings BO, which I have always weirdly loved. Shuddering, I open the windows and turn on the TV to kill the smells and the silence.

On the Food Network, Giada De Laurentiis is making exaggerated grimaces of delight as she stirs white wine into bubbling risotto in a soundstage apartment that probably smells like basil and cleaning products. I sit down in the same spot on the worn-out, once-white Ikea couch where I sat for four years, and I let the show completely entrance me for five minutes while a breeze from the street makes the rice-paper blinds I bought in Chinatown three years ago tap from side to side against the window frame. The cats finish eating the food I've given them and sidle up to the couch and sit with me and let me pet them, and for those five minutes it's like everything is back to normal.

In the car, my mom is talking on her hands-free device to Ms. Liu, who is a family therapist, about the moment when she became convinced that she and my dad were going to have to get a divorce. Actually, I don't know whether this is true, but it's possible. My parents are moving out of the house I grew up in next weekend and it's making both of them act crazy. My mom talked a lot about this last night, the idea of a divorce—it's true that my dad has made the whole move her problem and hasn't really acknowledged that she's leaving her job and her friends and her family to move to a totally new state with him. But there's no way she will ever really divorce him; I can tell when I ask her where she would live if they got divorced and she hasn't thought about that yet. Even I know that where you'll live is the first thing you think about, if you're serious about leaving.

Inside the apartment, one of the cats—the elder cat— starts to convulse. *Hork hork hork hork hork.* As I watch from the couch, I think about how, if the cat is dying, I'll have to call Joseph, who will come back from Boston and help me figure out what to do with a cat corpse (cremation?) and who will console me and be pretty fucking bummed himself—he loves the cats; that's always been one of my favorite things about him, how he says things to them like "Hey, little guy," which makes it seem like despite his midmorning joint-smoking and dead-end job he might be a good parent someday—and we'll cry together about the cat and then have consoling mutual-grief life-affirming sex. Or I could call the guy I cheated with. He would also console me and have sex with me—he's sort of vaguely obligated to—but he would not be bummed if the cat died. He's maybe allergic.

With a final *hork* the cat horks up a splattery hair ball and then that's over with.

My mom and I are back in the rental car, driving back to Daria's neighborhood. I scratch my arm absently and then I look down and notice that I have big raised bumps with wide white centers on my arm: being in my old apartment has made me break out in hives. The rental car has a pungent new-car smell and I can smell the BO and smoke still clinging to my skin in sharp opposition to it. My mom chatters blithely, either not noticing my discomfort or choosing to ignore it.

To get my mind off the apartment and my ex-boy-friend I start making myself think sexual thoughts, and then as long as I'm thinking about the guy I cheated with, I decide I might as well talk to my mom about him.

"So I started seeing this guy I really like."

She pauses for a minute and I can tell she's trying to figure out how to be diplomatic, which makes me resent whatever she's about to say already.

"Really?" is what she settles on, and of course her tone of voice somehow manages to convey, "Didn't you break up with your boyfriend who you'd been with for six years about four weeks ago?"

"Yeah and I really feel like it could be more than, like, a rebound thing. He's so different than anyone I've ever been with before. He's more like me in a way? He reads a lot of books. He likes to cook and he used to be a dancer and he has *Cooking for Mr. Latte* on his bookshelf. I'm making him sound gay, but he's actually really macho in this fascinating way?"

We're at a stoplight, and my mom is consulting the rental car's GPS, even though we're going back exactly the way we came. I scratch my arm.

"So what does he do?"

"The same thing I do."

"Where'd you meet him?"

"At work, Mom. He does the same thing I do."

We drive on in silence, with little rays of judgment radiating from my mom. Seriously, I can almost see them. Finally, in the same tone that she probably uses with the children whose court cases she represents for a living, she says, "I just think you should be careful right now. You're making a lot of changes fast and I just don't want you to get hurt by getting into something intense when you're just coming out of something intense, and I know that what you're doing feels good, right now, but . . . well, I'm not going to tell you what is or isn't a good idea. You have to figure this out for yourself."

I wish she would just say that she thinks I'm being an idiot and fucking up my life.

Or I wish she would tell me to stop what I'm doing. I wish someone would; I wish someone besides Joseph would care enough, ever, to do anything to prevent me from getting hurt besides saying "I don't want you to get hurt." But maybe this is not a realistic thing for an adult person to want.

"I don't think I'm going to get hurt, Mom," I say, realizing as I say it that I'm lying. But maybe it just feels like I'm lying because she puts me on the defensive.

On his bookshelves, the books are organized by the color of their spines. Even the air in the stairwell of his Lower East Side apartment building smells scrubbed and slightly plasticky, like coffee or the smell inside Crate & Barrel, and in the apartment it's colder still. Really, his apartment does seem a lot like a store, but it's unclear what might be for sale there. He and his roommate split the cost of weekly visits from a Vietnamese cleaning lady. The only other people I know who have a cleaning lady are my parents, and theirs only comes every other week.

He must have gotten up and cracked the door when he heard the buzzer, then returned to his seat at the far end of his long kitchen table. Now he's sitting there, typing on his laptop. I'm a little bit winded from walking up the stairs, and when I catch my breath my heart is still beating fast. I'm excited to see him, or maybe terrified. My heart won't slow down. I wish he'd gotten up to greet me. He looks up at me and smiles, closing his laptop. "We should make this quick. I have boxing practice in two hours," he says.

The cleaning lady hasn't visited his bedroom lately, from the looks of it. A huge pile of sweaty gym clothes clutters the bed, and he pushes them onto the floor so I can sit. Then he starts kissing me, smelling like good coffee and Kiehl's products, and it's what I've been thinking about all day but now it feels off. I'm suddenly aware of the bumps on my arm again—they'd been fine for a few hours but now they're back to itching. My stomach feels full of air. The inside of his mouth tastes scraped, like he's just flossed—blood and mint and coffee-staleness. But he's so ardent and pushy, more like a wrestler than a boxer, and he pins me eventually. I'm on the cusp of losing myself in it when suddenly up flashes the image of the older cat trembling and straining as he puked. I brush him aside and sit up. And then nothing works out exactly right.

Afterward, we sit on the fire escape half-naked and smoke a cigarette. Because he spends so much time working out, his smoking seems glamorous—louche and earned, not depressing and desperate like Joseph's. He passes the cigarette to me and looks away, letting the sunset kiss his profile and make him look like a still from a French movie, which is probably exactly what he's going for, but it still works. The day has cooled and now the air is the exact same temperature as the blood that's slowing its race through my veins. I slump against him and feel his body stiffen almost imperceptibly. He has five more minutes and then he really has to leave for boxing, and besides, sex never seems to relax him, nor does anything else.

I look in through the open window back into the room: the rumpled bed, my crumpled sundress. And then I look back at this guy, shirtless and with hardly any chest hair, and I understand suddenly that this is the last time I'll see him like this because doing this, again, with him would be like if you found a long black hair—not even a hair, a Band-Aid, a *fingernail*—in your lo mein and picked out the gross bit and kept eating. You'd have to be pretty hungry to do that.

Ten minutes later I'm in a cab headed back to Brooklyn, speeding over the bridge with the warm air rushing through the window, and my hair is whipping around my face, stinging my neck. There's only a tiny slice of sun left, and then even that slice disappears into East River and it's getting darker fast.

On our way into the park my mom and I notice a sign that says that dogs can go off-leash after 9 P.M. which it definitely is. We've been talking about moving: my new apartment, my parents' new apartment. These are chances for new starts, my mom says. Also: if my dad plays golf less often, she says, she will probably not divorce him. Lee trots on ahead of us energetically with her tongue hanging out of her mouth, focused, though it's not clear on what, exactly. Soon, my mom and I lapse into silence and start walking in the same lockstep.

"I wonder what would happen if we let her off the leash," I say eventually.

I stop walking, and so does Lee. My mom goes over and unclips the leash. Then we all start walking again, Lee a perfect leash-length ahead of us.

"Well, I guess that's what happens," I say after a while.

"Look at that," my mom says to Lee. "You're a metaphor."

7

Going Dutch

After I moved out of the Greenpoint apartment where Joseph and I had lived for four years and my monthlong sublet in the Beast House ended, I moved, alone, into a yearlong sublet in a rent-stabilized building on the southernmost edge of downtown Brooklyn.

The other tenants were all so old and infirm that you had to wonder how they negotiated the steep, crumbling stairs—mostly, it seemed, they didn't. They, or maybe the building itself, or possibly the construction site next door, were the source of a perpetual stench of damp rot that oozed through the floor-to-ceiling cracks in my apartment's peeling walls. But I lived there alone! I could do whatever disgusting thing I wanted at any time! For months before this became a source of terror and sadness, it felt like a delicious privilege. As long as the weather was warm enough to keep the windows open all the time, it definitely felt like a privilege. Being single, living alone, and working from home was an ongoing source of semi-gross, self-indulgent joy. I told Phillip this and he nodded sagely: "Just wait until the weather turns cold." I ignored him like I ignored everyone who wanted to criticize anything I was doing. For the moment, which was all that mattered, my life was full of a shrill, desperate kind of fun.

I was still working at Gawker but was getting more and more disgusted with the job and with myself. In the back of my mind I knew I would quit soon and so I felt very free, like nothing I did mattered anymore. Thinking about what I would do for a living after I'd left a job where I had professionally exploited and alienated every "connection" I'd ever had was too terrifying to contemplate, so I didn't contemplate it. I was also avoiding thinking about what would happen when I finally realized that Joseph and I were really not getting back together. This was also around the time that it was becoming unavoidably clear that my paternal grandfather in Long Island wasn't, at ninety, going to bounce back good as new from his latest bypass surgery. All kinds of doom were on the horizon, but I was determined to enjoy myself while I still could. Moments before someone dies of hypothermia, the internal organs give up and stop hoarding blood, so all that warm blood rushes back to the skin's surface at once and the sufferer tears off his clothing. That's what I was doing, I guess. It looked and even sometimes felt like exuberance. It's called "paradoxical undressing."

It was during this time I began "dating," that is, actually going out to dinner with semistrangers, for the first time. This might sound weird but you have to keep in mind that I had spent all of my early twenties sitting on the same couch with the same guy, getting high and making fun of the people on dating-themed reality shows. Perfect, then, that I was entering this complicated arena of human endeavor completely mindfucked, in terms of being able to invest myself sincerely in the life of another human being. I was not remotely over Joseph and still deeply ego-wounded from my intense Joseph-rebound crush's rejection. There was no way, in this state, that I would be capable of sustaining even the most superficial of "relationships." Somehow boys could smell this fundamental indifference on me. It's unsurprising, I guess, that they loved it.

Meanwhile, I had thought I would never have sex again. "I will never have sex again," I told my friends, who rolled their eyes. "I can't imagine feeling comfortable enough with anyone to want that. I will be completely alone for a *really long time*." This lasted a few weeks.

It was a Saturday night and I had just said good-bye to my parents, who had come to visit me and check out my new place, and also to visit my sick grandfather in Long Island. I had showed them around my apartment with pride; I think I'd thought they'd be impressed. They had been tactful. "It gets great light!" my mom said, looking out the window toward the tidy brownstones a block away, where I did not live. Earlier, in the car on the way back from a trip to the Brooklyn Heights promenade, she'd revealed that she'd been deeply insulted by some offhand comment I'd made a few months prior. Then, that night, we walked up and down Smith Street for half an hour, trying to find a restaurant that would seat us. I had neglected to make a reservation anywhere; I hadn't lived in the neighborhood long enough to understand the extent of its nesty, bourgie sceneyness. We ended up in a generic Italian restaurant's clamorous backyard. Just as our food arrived, my mom started talking about the months-prior inadvertent insult again and, in the same gradual way you realize you're going to vomit or sneeze, I realized that I was going to start crying. "Oh, cool," I thought. The pushy waiter came around to ask, "How is everything, folks," just as my tears began to drip into my already oversalted pasta.

We decided against dessert.

We walked back to my apartment in semisilence. My parents came in and walked me all the way up the smelly stairs to my front door, where at first it seemed that we would part like TV suitors after an unsuccessful date— them in the hallway, me inside, not inviting them in. But my dad asked if he could come inside and pee, and while he peed my mom hugged me and told me that she was proud of me, living here on my own, so grown up. It might have been my imagination that an unspoken "even though you are acting like a teenager" hung in the air between us.

I closed the door behind them and felt like crying again, but instead I called a car service to take me into the city, where I had to "cover" a party for work.

It was the last night of the long-running party thrown by the hipster DJs who called themselves the Misshapes, and the plan was to lurk with a staff videographer outside the West Village club where the party was being held and "interview" the revelers, whose ridiculous costumes Gawker's commenters would then be encouraged to mock. The club's staff chased us away from the entrance, so we had to do our lurking in a back alley. It turned out that this back alley wasn't a very popular route to the club's front door. Every fifteen minutes or so, someone in a keffiyeh or suspenders or a terry-cloth romper would walk by and refuse to talk to us.

Zack, the videographer, was just out of college. He

weighed maybe 120 pounds and habitually dressed a bit like the kids we were making fun of, in skintight pants and twenty-four hour Ray-Ban Wayfarer sunglasses. When no one came by for a while and we started getting bored, Zack asked about my day and I told him about my parents and my sick grandfather and the stupid fight and the crying at dinner. He told me about his fraught relationship with his parents and his recent breakup with a serious girlfriend, and he offered me a Xanax. I thought this was all very charming. A few minutes later he asked, in an offhand way, "Do you want to make out?"

I hadn't ever thought about this possibility, but once I had, I didn't bother to overthink it.

Zack seemed simultaneously very practiced and very teenagerishly enthusiastic, biting my lips and my neck. The biting was, I could tell, something someone else— probably the ex-girlfriend—had liked. In return, I kissed him the way Joseph had liked to be kissed. It was the only method of kissing I knew. I fixated on this for the first minute or so and then my reptile brain took over. We were just two reptiles, slithering over each other in an alley, getting slime on each other.

The next day he came over so we could review the footage we'd shot and decide how to edit it, which we did, for a while, and then we did some other stuff. It was very unusual—not entirely historically unprecedented, but nearly—for me to engage in this kind of stuff with-

out contextualizing the hookup as part of a larger narrative ("We are falling in love," "I am seducing him," "I
am being seduced," et cetera). What I was doing with
Zack, however, was not a story, it was just itself. After I
let him out of my apartment, I went in the bathroom and
inspected the bruises on my neck, smiled at myself in the
mirror, then went back to my desk and finished up the
workday without another thought about it. That night,
I had a date—a first date with a friend of a friend. It was
for all intents the first date of my adult life. We met for
drinks, which he paid for, at a bar near my house.

Daniel was tall, with close-cropped hair and a small
nose that made him seem, despite his masculine bearing, cute in the way the creatures in the Small Mammal
House at the zoo are cute. We had met at a party months
earlier, and I'd remembered him and initiated a volley
of flirtatious Facebook messages. He had some sort of
do-gooderish job for the city that required him to wear
suits, and he had come straight from work to our date,
so he was wearing a suit. I was wearing the same jeans
and T-shirt that I wear pretty much every day. We talked
about work and I kept making jokes where at first he'd
look at me with a look of shocked incomprehension and
then he'd decide to start laughing. But mostly he was
very comfortable to be around, despite seeming slightly
nervous. His attraction to me was palpable in his ner-
vousness, which made him attractive.

Drinks went well enough that we decided to have dinner in the backyard of a nondescript Southeast Asian restaurant a few blocks farther down Atlantic. It turned out that he had traveled in Southeast Asia, so a lot of our dinner conversation consisted of me encouraging him to describe his travels. It was nice to feel that I had the upper hand and could basically instruct him to entertain me with stories. At the end of an anecdote I could hear the indrawn breath and see the tension in his jaw as he waited to see my reaction, and after I noticed this I started deliberately withholding each of my "uh-huh"s and encouraging half-laughs for a second. He didn't order a drink with dinner, so I didn't either. We split the check. As we were leaving he told me that he was having such a good time he didn't want the evening to be over, not in a sleazy way but in a spirit of quiet resignation like, "Oh, but alas, it is over." I pointed out that I lived very nearby and asked him, unblinking, if he would like to come up for coffee, although I didn't have any coffee.

In my apartment, not drinking coffee, Daniel was too nice. As we kissed he kept *looking* at me, like, trying to catch my eye, and when he did the look he gave me was wide-open and sweet. When he touched me his hands were tentative and their movements seemed motivated by therapeutic intent, like he was giving a backrub to my front. None of this was particularly erotic, but I was in a state, and in retrospect it's hard to know whether he felt like a lucky beneficiary or a frightened observer of this state. I don't think it was really so much that he was scared, but more that he was trying to be proper, to preserve at least the idea that he was the more rapacious of the two of us. After a long above-the-belt while, he excused himself by saying, basically, that he wanted to leave before he was tempted to do something he'd regret because he "liked me" and therefore "wanted to take things slow." In the moment I was charmed by this, but after he left I thought it over with a cooler head and realized that Daniel and I were at cross-purposes. He seemed to want a girlfriend. Underlying everything he'd said, even the things he'd passively communicated to me via his Facebook profile—the photos with animals, bicycles, and children—was this message: "I am ready to have a girlfriend." And I'd been attracted to this because of, I think, brainwashing. But when I stopped to think about it—lying in bed, in the exact center of the bed, occupying as much space in the bed as I wanted, I thought about it—I realized that I did not want to be Daniel's or anyone's girlfriend. Not remotely.

But I still went out on another date with him, because I did want something from him and I was curious to see whether I could get it, and what it would be like if I did. In the interim, I created excuses to shoot videos for work with Zack again.

As a child I was a little bit disgusted and embarrassed to learn about the facts of life, and did not immediately connect the idea of "sex" to the feelings I got when I lay on the carpet on my stomach, idly humping a stuffed animal while watching *Sesame Street*. The revelation that sex could be something to anticipate happily rather than to dread as another unpleasant grown-up duty came to me, eventually, in a dream. Nothing overtly sexual even happened in this dream—it was a dream about the feeling of lying in bed on a sunny afternoon with sun streaking the sheets, surrounded by warmth, feeling satisfied. It took a long time for life to catch up to this idealized vision of what sex could be like; it's still not like that every time, but when it is, I notice.

Bored and at loose ends one night, I went over to Zack's apartment to watch HBO on his huge TV. He lived in one of those prefab new buildings in Williamsburg that's full of rich recent college graduates who personalize their apartments with cast-off furniture from their parents' rec rooms. Inevitably in these places there is a leather sectional sofa, a big flat-screen, and either nothing or dorm-style posters on the walls. After we spent an hour watching *Curb Your Enthusiasm* with his roommate, we retired to the bedroom. There we enacted a ritual that is so familiar to me that I think there should be a name for it: the moment when the girl, still semiclothed, lies in bed, and the boy jumps out of bed to hunch over his computer and scroll through his iTunes to select the perfect sound track. Inevitably he hovers there, deliberating, for about thirty seconds too long, so that the girl has a chance to examine his shirtless torso, unflatteringly hunched and compressed, unflatteringly lit by the screen's blue glow. What a relief, finally, to hear those first few strains of Air or My Bloody Valentine and to be able to close your eyes and let yourself be lulled back into complacency by the warm comfort of familiar melodies and the familiar feeling of skin on skin.

Afterward we lay in bed and talked and laughed until late at night, just like people who are falling in love but without any of the fraught intensity or self-conscious-ness that people who are falling in love feel. How ideal, I thought, and remembered my childhood dream of happy sex. In the future I hoped that all my conquests would be like this. Everything was much easier, it turned out, when you didn't care about the person in bed with you. I was shocked that it had taken me so long to figure this out.

Before I got a chance to go on a second date with Daniel he showed up, uninvited, at a Gawker party. It was a weekday, so he was in his suit, a fancy pin-striped one, and he was wearing glasses with earnest (as opposed to ironic) thick black frames. He stood next to me and touched my shoulder in a way that probably gave people the impression that we were together. He must have noticed that I bristled. I could see no solution but to pretend I was leaving the party with him, but what I really did was walk him to the subway, kiss him good-bye, then walk back to the party by myself. I didn't see him again, but I did note that a few months later his Facebook status changed to "in a relationship," and I was glad that someone else had wanted to be his girlfriend.

The next night there was another party. It seemed like there were an unprecedented number of parties that fall. It was fun and unfamiliar to go to these parties with an agenda I hadn't had since college. I had forgotten, during all those years of having a boyfriend, the reason that people go to parties. My particular agenda at this party, which was being held by a small literary magazine, was to seduce one of the magazine's former interns—a recent college graduate named Alexei—and to gather enough information about the party to make fun of it on Gawker. I had never met Alexei before, but we'd e-mailed each other in a professional capacity, and I'd heard rumors about his cuteness.

The party was held in the magazine's tiny office on the Lower East Side, a narrow space that was almost unbearably overheated by all the bodies it contained. Alexei was busy circulating, and I only knew two other people at the party: one author whose book party I'd written up and another author whose novel I'd studied in a college erotica workshop. I went over and stood near them and reintroduced myself and laughed overloudly at everything they said, trying to seem at ease and not out of place. I needed a drink. There were bottles of Brooklyn Lager in a bucket behind a makeshift bar, and a guy, who turned out to be the editor of the magazine, was there uncapping them for people. As he uncapped one for me we flirted a little, and for a moment I was distracted from my mission. He wasn't really my type—compact and muscular, with chest hair pushing past the top button of his polo shirt—but I liked that he knew who I was.

But then Alexei was leaving; his friend had a car and they had room to give me a ride to the next party, in somebody's backyard in Brooklyn. In the car I sat squished between him and somebody else, and I pressed my thigh into Alexei as we rounded every turn. He seemed to press back. In the backyard, though, we lost track of each other; I ran into someone I knew and got wrapped up in a conversation, and the next time I looked at my phone it was three o'clock.

I didn't see Alexei anywhere so I walked out into the street in front of the brownstone to try and hail a cab. Darting my head from side to side to scan the street, I caught a glimpse of a white shirt in the distance, and a girl's dark hair: Alexei and a pale, moonfaced girl, deep in a conversation that did not look romantic, exactly, but still, there they were. A cab rounded the corner and as I stepped into it Alexei looked up from his conversation and caught my eye. I gave him a blank smile, then ducked into the car and closed the door. When the driver asked where I was headed I told him to just go north while I figured it out. I texted Zack. A second later, he replied that he was awake and didn't mind at all if I came over.

I had been drinking slowly but steadily over the course of the evening and had gotten to that unfun plateau of drunkenness that is indistinguishable from sobriety in all its particulars except that you can feel that you will eventually have a headache. I was frustrated, and Zack was a handy container for any kind of feelings I was having about any boys or, really, anyone. I closed my eyes and he became anyone.

As the sunrise began to slant through the bedsheet hung curtain-style over Zack's window, I thought about Flaubert's journal of his travels in Egypt, the part where he catalogues and qualifies the sex acts performed during a night spent with a belly-dancing courtesan: the first ribald, the next frantic, the final act tender. My own night had been so long and I was still so incredibly awake, as was Zack. We finally took some of his Xanax and reached for each other one more time as it began to take effect. I don't know how Flaubert would have described this final session but to me it felt like the borders of our hard, thin bodies were turning blurry, melting into each other. The physical warmth and fuzziness almost compensated for the emotional lack of same. Earlier in my nonrelationship with Zack I had thought that one of the great things about what we were doing was that I would never know when we were doing what we were doing for the last time ever. But this did not turn out to be true.

After a few hours of fitful sleep I called the same car service and stood outside of Zack's house waiting for the car, wearing sunglasses, watching a parade of moms walk down his block hand in hand with their toddlers. When the car came I rolled down the window so that the air-freshener trees wouldn't turn my stomach and kept it rolled down even as we zoomed around the curves of the BQE at roller-coaster speed. I got an egg sandwich at the deli downstairs from my apartment and sprinted up the stairs, and while I attacked the sandwich I checked my e-mail. There was an e-mail from Alexei that he'd sent at 4 A.M. He had gone home alone, was the subtext. He wondered if I was free for dinner that night. I supposed I was, but first I had to take a shower and a nap.

A few weeks later I woke up next to Alexei in my grubby apartment and lay there, frozen in place. I had to get up and go get on the Long Island Railroad and visit my grandfather in the hospital, but all these feelings I had thought I'd left behind in the Greenpoint apartment with Joseph were seeping in through the cracks in the walls here. My heart was heavy but somehow it still pounded too fast, no matter how slowly I breathed, no matter how hard I willed it to slow down. I rolled over and curled up against Alexei's chest but didn't feel comforted. He woke up; he stroked my back. He offered to go with me, and I think he really would have gone. The sunlight on his face made him look even younger. He rolled over and went back to sleep as I stood in front of the mirror over my dresser, applying concealer to the circles under my eyes.

They had recently remodeled the hospital, and the drama that day was about whether my grandfather would be moved from a room in the old wing to a room in the new wing. The vulnerable details of his body embarrassed me: the waxy buildup in his ears, the gray bristles unevenly studding his chin. Up until a few years ago he'd gotten regular manicures, the old-fashioned masculine kind where they buff the nails to a stony matte gleam. Now his untrimmed toenails poked crescents in his socks. His feet in general, sticking out from under the covers at the end of the bed, looked purely ornamental, and it turned out to be true that he would not stand on them again. But on this visit he could still sit up, and smile, and complain in a way that seemed imperious, not pathetic. My aunt and my grandmother and I had a small fight about whether or not it was worth paying the fee to turn on the room's TV set, considering that he might end up getting moved to a different room and we would have to pay the fee again. I drank constantly from a bottle of water in order to have something to do, and so I kept having to pee. All day my hands reeked of hospital-grade antibacterial soap. Every time I pulled down my pants I looked down at my naked thighs with a mixture of revulsion and gratitude. Goose bumped and pale in the air-conditioning, my legs still looked so young and alive that I could hardly believe they belonged to me. When my grandfather had to pee he gruffly asked us to turn away, then turned to the side and peed into one of those kidney-shaped receptacles. I pinned my eyes to the topmost corner of the window, which looked out on a rooftop and a blank new wall. I guess there had been a view of something else from this room at one point, but it had been supplanted by a view of the new wing.

I had told Alexei I would call him when I got home, but he wasn't the person I wanted to call. Joseph had met my grandparents dozens of times; he would know exactly what it meant to me that my grandfather was dying. He knew that I was ashamed of them for being as openly obsessed with status and accomplishments as I secretly was, and that I'd felt as though my status and accomplishments had been a perpetual disappointment to them. He knew that no matter how much I made fun of their accents and their snobbish opinions of movies they hadn't seen, I loved them in a way I loved few other people.

They had always seemed invincible, larger than life—I had never imagined that they would die, which, considering how old they were, was pretty shortsighted of me. I had never imagined having to go to my grandfather's funeral but I was imagining it now, and I discovered that in my imagination Joseph was standing there next to me.

So when I got home I called Joseph. I hadn't spoken to him since I'd picked up the last of my things four months prior. I told him about the hospital et cetera. He cut me off; he had a bone to pick with me about something I'd written on Gawker about "going Dutch" on a date. This was insensitive to him, he said, that I would write something about how I was dating. I apologized even though I didn't feel sorry. Hadn't half the point of breaking up with him been that I would now no longer have to consider how he'd feel about what I wrote? He grudgingly accepted my apology and then we talked in a civil but distant way about the details of my grandfather's illness for a few minutes, the way you'd talk about that kind of thing to a solicitous stranger.

Soon we got off the phone. It was bizarre to get off the phone without saying "I love you," or calling him "baby." It seemed unlikely that I would ever say those things to anyone else, either. My life from now on was going to be just waking up in strangers' beds and making my way from there to a beloved relative's funeral alone, basically.

I lay down on my bed, feeling suddenly chilled. The weather had gotten cooler during the previous few days, and my cantankerous building's radiators were still stone-cold to the touch. Instead of getting up and putting on a sweater, though, I just lay there, waiting for my limbs to start going numb, but they never did.

8

Hopey

No one thought it was a good idea for me to get a puppy, not even me, really. I'd even named the dog Hopey, as if freighting this tiny animal with a huge and obvious symbolic meaning would guarantee her a place in my heart. Instead it was like the time Joseph got me a potted marantha for Valentine's Day and I joked that it was "the plant of our love" and then, having said that, I felt obligated to keep the stupid love-plant alive for years. The plant finally made good on its longtime efforts to die with help from Joseph, whose refusal to water it after I left was probably more laziness than symbolic gesture, and then more than a year later I found out that maranthas are so sensitive to fluoride that you're only supposed to water them with bottled water or rainwater. That would explain why the plant of our love spent its life at death's door, pale leaves perpetually curling and brown around the edges. I suppose I could have Googled care instructions for maranthas back when it still mattered, but then, I could have done a lot of things differently.

The sky was steely and bleak and the scenery was even bleaker on the drive out to the breeder's house in New Jersey. My friend Vivian's rusty Honda sailed over bridges and under overpasses that looked the same for miles and miles. Everything seemed to be made out of concrete, everything was wet and gray. It was the kind of winter day when there's no morning or afternoon, just a perpetual four o'clock. Under normal circumstances the mere sight of Vivian's car, with its tape deck full of ten-year-old mixes, would cheer me up, but circumstances hadn't been normal for a while, for a month or so at least. A few minor life-catastrophes, each manageable on its own, had piled up on me. Then the weight of the pile had settled just above my breastbone, leaving me incapable of experiencing anything besides boredom and pain—the kind of pain that's basically just boredom, sharpened and concentrated.

That kind of pain is almost as boring to hear about

as it is to experience, but I knew Vivian wouldn't mind
if I treated her to the whole litany, and anyway it was a
long car ride. So I gave her a status update: I'd been to
another doctor, a urologist with lots of Viagra posters in
his office, about the weird constant pain low in my stomach, but still nobody had any idea what was going on.
My grandfather's funeral the previous week had been,
you know, how funerals are. I'd spent it mostly feeling
guilty for not being able to stop thinking, during all the
speeches and graveside weeping, about how unfair it was
that Joseph didn't have to be there, holding my hand and
talking to me so I wouldn't have to talk to my relatives. I
had loved my grandfather, whose decline and death had
been protracted and wrenching. Also, I'd just quit my
job at Gawker to "freelance," which so far had meant
staying in bed as long as possible in the mornings, clinging to the last shreds of unconciousness until I'd run out
of feverish half-dreams, then finding some random thing
to do until enough time had passed that I could get back
into bed and sleep again.

Vivian nodded sagely and told me about how over-
loaded she was with work and the cold she was having trouble shaking, and then we tried to puzzle out the
Mapquest directions. She didn't say any of the obvious
dumb stuff like: you need to snap out of it. Stop feeling
sorry for yourself. She didn't even really mention the dog
except to say, "Well, you'll have to get out of bed in the

morning to walk the dog," and I was like "Yeah," and then we lapsed into silence, listening to the low hiss of the tape deck spinning its empty wheels and the whoosh of the highway.

Half an hour later we were pulling up at this low ranch house where you could smell dog from the end of the driveway. The smell got stronger when a little herd of adult shih tzus greeted us at the door, jumping at our legs and manically rolling their gooey-looking black eyes. One of them got so excited that she headed to the corner, ignoring a Wee-Wee Pad spread on the ominously stained carpet, and took a shit.

She looked up at us expectantly.

There was a framed portrait of a heroic shih tzu on the wall, done in craft-store acrylic paint. The breeder ushered us through the living room into the kitchen, making cooing noises at the dogs. The kitchen had a pass-through window into the living room, so we could see the shit in the corner still sitting there, stinking.

But then there was Hopey, tiny and categorically adorable in the way of all baby animals. She was romping around in a pen lined with newsprint, playing with her littermates. Her fur was black and pristine white, and her beady eyes shone in her cute, squished-in face. She was a little bit bigger than a foot-long sub. I picked her up and held her, her soft canine warmth reassuring in my arms. When I set her down she started yelping—loud, high-pitched, birdlike cries. "Pick her back up, Mommy! She wants her mommy already!" cried the breeder. I wrote that psycho a check as quickly as I could and we left, Hopey yelping but safe in the special expensive soft-sided carrier I'd bought for her. I stroked her absently and whispered to her to calm down, wondering when the transformation would take place. I hoped it would be soon.

But over the course of the next few days, I kept not starting to love her. I had bought all the books about what to expect from your new puppy, but I'd only ever taken care of friends' adult dogs before, wise-eyed creatures with mature, fully formed personalities who could be counted on to spend most of their days lazing on their doggie beds. Hopey repeatedly brought the baby gates I'd bought to keep her in the noncarpeted part of the apartment crashing down on her own tiny head and then rushed to the kitchen to gulp down her body weight in cat food, which she would then digest and poop out at unpredictable intervals, in unpredictable locations—including inside her crate, which the puppy books had claimed she'd never soil. She spent her outdoor time shivering and trying to eat rocks and pieces of tinfoil but never going—as the puppy books suggested I call it—"potty." "Go potty. Go potty," I implored, as the tiny dog quivered miserably and passersby shot me horrified looks.

I broke down and bought the Wee-Wee Pads. Whatever socialization had happened at the breeder's house had included a set of ingrained rules that I was not about to be able to break. I was not Cesar Millan the Dog Whisperer. I wasn't even really a dog person. I had always been an animal lover, tenderhearted to a fault as a child, ruining the other kids' caterpillar-squishing, slug-salting fun, throwing traps full of crabs back into the ocean to save them from boiling. But I felt no tenderness toward my own dog; that potentially tender part of me felt numb. I would sit, tossing a chewy toy for Hopey to retrieve with all the bored perfunctory zeal of an underpaid day-care aide, counting the throws, wishing I could find a button that would turn her off. I tried to imagine the cheerier person who, several months prior, had initially contacted the breeder. She seemed like a complete stranger.

Two weeks in, I had to face facts: I wasn't even falling in like. My idea of fun was lying facedown in bed occasionally turning my head to stare at the wall. Hopey's idea of fun was biting everything that moved—she was probably teething—and terrorizing the cat. Raffles, previously proud and extroverted, had ceded his rights to the apartment and now spent most of his days crouched under furniture, wearing a facial expression I'd only ever seen before in photographs of prisoners at the end of a forced march. Hiding would never have occurred to

Hopey. She refused to be ignored—if I turned away from her for a second to look at the computer screen, she'd bark nonstop for ten minutes before finally distracting herself by finding some dangerous electrical object to chew on. And there were plenty; the apartment was full of hazards. The apartment was hazardous to every living being in it, especially me.

Inarguably, I was in a bad place mentally, but as so often happens, I was simultaneously in a bad place, apartmentwise. I'd found the sublet during the summer, at the height of my postbreakup manic phase, and my rose-tinted view had made the top floor of the dilapidated tenement building—improbably big, improbably cheap—seem not just desirable, but ideal. Okay, it had peeling paint and crumbling linoleum and permanently filthy carpet tacked clumsily over rotting, roach-infested floorboards, but these things—sometimes called "character"—were unavoidable in New York, right? Unavoidable, that is, unless you wanted to move into one of those cheesy new-construction rental towers, the housing equivalent of Ikea furniture. That exact kind of cheesy building was rising on every side of my tenement. A smarter shopper might have observed this and surmised, correctly, that my landlord would be uninterested in making basic repairs or performing routine exterminations, preferring instead to slowly frustrate his elderly, rent-stabilized tenants out of their homes and then sell his property to developers who would knock it down and build another Ikea tower. But it was summer, and what did I care? Whenever I got sick of the apartment's character, I could just walk over to the Brooklyn Heights promenade and stare across the water and feel like I was in a movie.

Then the weather turned colder and my precarious, artificial happiness started to fall apart. The apartment fell apart too, less gradually. An inexplicable deathy smell sometimes filled the bedroom, emanating, perhaps, from one of the floor-to-ceiling cracks in the wall. The shower, whose tiny head was held in place by twisted wire hangers—a makeshift apparatus that gave the bather the sensation of being gently peed on—stopped running hot. The roaches ignored the traps and bait I put out for them and boldly scampered around the kitchen at all hours, and then they got so bold they left the kitchen. One day I watched one of them lose its footing while climbing my bedroom wall, only to land softly in the sheets of my unmade bed. How could I have brought another living being into these degraded circumstances? That night, as I lay awake, listening to Hopey bark and whine herself to fitful sleep, I imagined roaches crawling unchecked across my sleeping face. Sleep had been the only pleasure left to me, and even that was ruined now. I got out of bed and led Hopey to her Wee-Wee Pad. "Go potty," I said. "Go potty. Go potty?" She took the edge of the pad between her teeth and shook it, growling.

The next day I went to Greenpoint to visit a friend who had recently moved in with her boyfriend. The boyfriend wasn't at home, but their apartment still had that muzzy couple-y feeling, that smell of boy laundry and girl perfume that's almost a vague echo of sex. It was Christmastime and her boyfriend had bought a white plastic light-up Christmas tree on a whim and set it up in their TV room, she told me, and then they'd basked in its tacky elegance, kissing, probably, and laughing. To get home, I had to get on the subway at the end of my old block, and once I was that close I figured I might as well stand on the sidewalk outside my old first-floor apartment and imagine our living room as I'd left it—the walls painted Ralph Lauren "Surfboard Yellow," the '70s rec-room landscape paintings salvaged from the sidewalk, the rocking chair, the battered couch. There were so many things I hadn't taken with me when I left, and so many things I couldn't have taken with me—the way those yellow walls reflected lamplight, for example, or the way the sun came in through the torn rice-paper window shades, the ones I'd bought in Chinatown, the ones I could see, from the street outside, still hanging where I'd left them. Who knew what else in the apartment was the still the same? Possibly nothing.

The lights were on. I still had keys, even. I could have just walked in the door. Instead, I walked back to the subway. I had to get home to feed my dog.

In retrospect it's amazing to me that at that low point in my life—when I was depressed, unemployed, and also, scarily, seemingly unemployable, afflicted with a mysterious, chronically painful medical condition (it turned out to be something called "interstitial cystitis," which is exactly as sexy as it sounds), living in a hovel with an extremely unendearing pet, I managed to maintain something that passed for a romantic relationship. Alexei appeared outside the smelly vestibule of the tenement building, bearing a box set of *Twin Peaks* and a toy for Hopey to sink her tiny, razor-sharp fangs into. We talked about our recent breakups and then crawled into my bed to have the kind of escapist sex that you never want to end in the same way that you never want an engrossing trashy movie that you're watching stoned while compulsively eating from a box of Junior Mints to end.

Sex inevitably does end, though, and whenever it did I'd be worse off than before, back in reality, in my terrible roach-bed, realizing that I was just as alone with Alexei there as I'd been before he came over. He was four years my junior but at the time that felt like a life-time. Once I wore a tank top and he told me it made me look "younger" and then didn't understand why I was mad. For my part, I couldn't understand why I kept not falling in love with him. He was brilliant and prom-ising—he had precociously landed and speedily made a name for himself in a difficult, prestigious job—and he was beautiful, with big soulful eyes and one of those gangly, boyish bodies girls love because it inspires desire and protectiveness simultaneously. He was so young that even after smoking half a pack of cigarettes and staying up all night the inside of his mouth tasted like some mild fruit. His hair was smooth and floppy and baby-soft, just like Hopey's.

I got rid of the dog first.

I had spent another weekday alone, walking the cold streets of my neighborhood aimlessly, watching the patches of sky between the branches of the bare trees go from gray to dusky black. When evening came I duti-fully dragged myself through a yoga class at the YMCA, and then at the end of it, as we lay on the floor in corpse pose, a series of images of the future came rushing at me unbidden. I imagined Hopey, full-size, still shitting on pads, pads still lining the hallway of my horrific apart-ment. And then, for some reason, and for the first time, I imagined Joseph with another girl. I was pricking myself purposely with the thought, and it worked. I rushed out of the classroom, the tears in my eyes making it difficult to tie my shoes. I waited until I was outside the gym to start weeping in earnest, and then I cried all the way home. I cried as I climbed the four flights of dusty stairs to my apartment, and I kept crying as I was greeted by Hopey, who yelped and leapt and nipped at my legs. I hunched over and knelt on the hallway linoleum and she climbed into my lap and let me hold her as my tears fell onto her. But then she squirmed out of my arms, and a minute later I heard the crash as one of the baby gates fell.

For a terrible moment I found myself hoping that it had crushed her skull, and then I heard her slurping cat food in the kitchen and felt ashamed and relieved, and then I walked over to my computer and sent the breeder an e-mail, explaining that Hopey had not hit it off with my cat, and though it broke my heart to have to return her, I had to respect Raffle's seniority in the household. As soon as I hit send, I felt better than I had in months.

It was Friday, and the plan was for Vivian to come over in the morning to drive back out to New Jersey with Hopey and all her toys. I had already bagged them all up, along with her food, her food bowls, and her Wee-Wee Pads. I took her outside for one last sprinting, trash-gobbling walk, not entirely ruling out the chance that we'd have some kind of moment when I'd look into her black eyes and have a change of heart. Either that, or I would start to feel regret or some kind of sadness about what I was about to do. But by then, it turned out, I was too sad in general to be vulnerable to any specific sadness.

We wrapped up our walk and stood outside the front door to play Go Potty for the last time. I gave up easily. "I'll miss you," I told her, insincerely. She bit down on a foil gum wrapper and chewed it ruminatively. "No. That's not food." I stuck my finger into her tiny mouth and fished it out. At least she hadn't killed herself on my watch, despite her many attempts to do so. That was something, at least.

Alexei had come over the previous evening. I'd tried to put him off, but he'd called and said that he had to talk to me. When I greeted him downstairs (the apartment had no buzzer), he looked very somber, and the small talk we made as we climbed the four flights of stairs felt more strained than usual. He didn't take off his shoes or his coat when we walked into the apartment, past the pile of Hopey's things. We walked into my bedroom, where, a few months earlier, the alien version of me who'd been susceptible to emotions had first invited him in on the pretext of examining my bookshelves. Now he pressed his face to mine, the tip of his nose as cold as the air outside, then pulled away to look at me with a pained expression. I wished he would leave; I felt too exhausted for a dramatic scene. I wasn't interested in hurting his feelings, but I wasn't up to feigning any feelings of my own. "This isn't working," he said, with the naive conviction of a soap-opera actor. "You're right," I said, relieved. But it wasn't over. He talked about how my ambivalence toward him—my refusal to decide whether or not he was properly my "boyfriend"—was hurting him. Didn't I care about him? I did, I said. "If I was capable of having those kinds of feelings right now, I would have them for you," I said, sincerely enough, looking past his left shoulder at the crack in the wall behind him.

He grabbed the sides of my face and held them between his long, cold hands, forcing me to look straight into his eyes, and he was wide open to me in a way that you can only be when you're twenty-three and it's only the first or second or third time you've done this.

And then it was there, the feeling I had hoped for. Something in my chest came open and the weight, for a moment, was dislodged by a warm flush that rose up, heating my cheeks under the touch of his cold hands.

I smiled at him, and he smiled back, and we kissed, then, hopefully. But somewhere in the middle of the kiss the feeling drained away as quickly as it had welled up.

On the drive out to New Jersey the next morning I held Hopey in her carrier on my lap, feeling her warm weight on me for the last time. She seemed thrilled, when we arrived, to be reunited with her dog family. She and her siblings immediately romped off together to some redolent carpeted corner of the ranch house in search of electrical cables to chew on.

I let her go without saying good-bye, a word that, like her own name and "potty," I was pretty sure she didn't comprehend at all. "Oh, it's so sad," the breeder kept saying. "When your cat crosses the rainbow bridge, you'll come back and get another puppy."

9

And the Heart Says

We had a long conversation before we left about whether we would bring any pot with us to the Bethany Beach condo my parents were letting us stay in for a week. I had voted at first for not bringing any, but then I'd changed my mind and decided we should just bring a little bit. Just a little bit, and probably we wouldn't even smoke it, but we'd bring it anyway so that we wouldn't feel panicky—it would make us feel better just to know that we had it. Unless we got pulled over, in which case it would not make us feel better at all, but we would drive the speed limit and generally not do anything stupid. We were going to be very responsible. Weird, a little, that going on vacation alone together felt like the most responsible and grown-up thing we'd ever done.

We took photos, which was rare. I still hardly ever take photos; I hate the way they interfere with actual memory. My memories of that week are an imaginary pile of snapshots alongside the ones we took: the one Joseph took of me in my gold and black suit—one running toward the water, and then another one after the swim with shiny line of salt water trickling down my stomach. And the ones I took, the one of Joseph's naked shoulders rising up from a beach blanket, the one of Joseph squinting into the sun and smiling, about to bite into a breakfast burrito on the boardwalk. The imaginary snapshots are along the same lines but more explicit. We were twenty-four.

After we came back to New York the glow of this vacation stayed with us for weeks, during which we cut back our pot intake significantly and Joseph came with me to yoga class for the first time. I remember walking down 4th Street between First and A with him after class, holding hands, saying, "Thank you." He said no problem, his pleasure, he'd enjoyed the class, he was going to start going all the time. The next week, though, he had band practice, and the week after there was some other conflict, and also without noticing it we were back to smoking pot every day again as the days grew shorter and

I started staying later at work again and then—without even noticing what we were losing—we had lost whatever we'd had that week at the beach. A sense of possibility, mostly. I remember standing in the little bathroom in the beach apartment and thinking for the first time that Joseph and I could get married, that marriage was a possible thing that could happen to me. The future was still unclear, but just unclear enough to be exciting and not so unclear as to be frightening. I felt then that I understood for the first time what people were after, vis-à-vis love. I felt like the literal heart in my chest was wrapped in layers of warm cotton batting that were keeping it safe. This feeling wasn't fake, even though it turned out to be temporary.

Three years later my parents put their furniture in storage and moved into that beach condo for a few months while they looked at apartments in DC and Maryland, near where I grew up. My dad's job had taken him to—and then, abruptly, away from—a two-year sojourn in Miami that had never seemed quite real. Because their stay at the beach place would only be for a few months, I had hoped to avoid a visit, but when my mom asked directly, I had trouble explaining to her why I didn't want to go.

"I remember the scratchy polyester of the pineapple-printed comforter in the master bedroom, rough against my face at the foot of the bed in the middle of the day." I guess I could have told her that. "Every minute I spend there, I will be working not to remember that." Instead I said, "Okay."

I took the train out of town in the afternoon, arriving just in time for Passover seder at my aunt's house. We woke up in Maryland the next morning, and my mom and I visited my maternal grandparents' retirement community before we embarked on our drive over and across to the coast.

"She is a love," my grandfather told us when my mom asked how my grandmother was doing. She had been diagnosed with Alzheimer's a few months earlier. My grandfather, by contrast, was as always preternaturally healthy. In the '50s he'd moved the family to Uganda so he could take aerial photographs of cattle migration patterns, and at eighty-nine he couldn't be prevented from spending one day a week pruning vines and measuring soil chemical composition at the vineyard in southern Maryland he'd been tending for the past thirty years. He began telling us some of the latest details of my grandmother's decline while I absently played with the tiles of a word game on the table. Then she arrived home from her exercise class unexpectedly.

I hadn't seen her since the diagnosis. She looked

softer, somehow, and her face was more abstracted, like a child's. She felt softer when I hugged her. "We were just talking about you," I admitted, because I thought it seemed so obvious that it was awkward not to acknowledge it. She smiled and asked what we'd said about her, and to my surprise my grandfather answered matter-of-factly. He touched her head then, the same way he had touched the top of my head when I was a child. He has never been a hugging type of person and he would make a joke about that, when I was little, by greeting me and my cousins by describing what he was doing: "Pat, pat," he would say.

We ate lunch at the retirement home's restaurant-cum-cafeteria, where my grandparents were entitled to a meal a day as part of their rent. My mother and I both ordered the salmon niçoise salad, which was a mistake, and as we picked leaves of lettuce out from underneath the gluey dressing we talked about my cousin's upcoming wedding. The wedding had been a focus of conversation at the Seder the previous night, and some part of me was still feeling stung by the knowledge that nothing I had yet accomplished, and maybe nothing I would ever accomplish, would be able to provoke the same kind of unambiguous, categorical approval from my family. This is a dumb way to think, obviously. My grandfather asked me how I felt about getting married and I said some things about wanting to be able to be a complete person on my own and having problems with the "bourgeois, patriarchal" institution itself. "Is that okay with you?"

"It's fine, but we do want grandchildren," my grandmother said. "I *am* grandchildren!" I said. "Great-grandchildren," she corrected herself. It wasn't clear whether she had misspoken or had been confused; I wanted to think it was the former. I told her not to discount the possibility that my brother or eldest male cousin "could knock someone up." I became conscious of acting like an asshole and tried to be conciliatory. "I'm not saying that it will never happen. Just stay alive."

After lunch we went to see my grandfather's plot in the retirement village's communal gardens, where he took a knife out of his pocket and cut off a head of lettuce that was growing in his cold frame, then put it in a plastic bag and gave it to us to take to the beach. After this we walked down a path to one of the village's man-made ponds, where a man was sitting on a bench in front of a pile of dried corn that he'd scattered to try to entice the two swans that were swimming there.

The male was smaller and he stayed in the pond. The female got out of the pond and advanced toward me as I stood on the bank throwing corn. She darted her head, moving her long prehensile neck like a snake toward the corn in my hand, and I jumped and backed away. My mom called to me from the parking lot, telling me that it was almost time to go. I walked over to where my grandparents and mother were standing in the parking lot, and then we went and got in the car.

The story of the beginning of my relationship with Joseph is so familiar to me that it's boring to tell it; this is because I evolved a pat version of it over the course of our six-year relationship that I would tell when asked, "So how did you guys meet?" In telling this version I would focus on the cutesy detail of: when I first moved to New York my roommates and I didn't have a TV and so we would go over to the apartment of Joseph and his roommates, who did. Their apartment was on 9th Street between C and D, in one of those newly built buildings where the boxy apartments are subdivided into three or four cubby-size bedrooms and a common room with just enough space for the smallest-size couch Ikea makes. After a month of visits accompanied by my roommates, I walked over to the 9th Street apartment alone for the first time, without a TV show as a pretext. Joseph buzzed me up and as I walked in the door the Byrds album *Sweetheart of the Rodeo* was beginning to play its first cut, a cover of Bob Dylan's "You Ain't Goin' Nowhere." The next morning I walked home to my own cubby on 3rd Street, filled with the kind of irrational euphoria that I had until then only read about in women's magazines. It made no sense, and I knew it made no sense, but I was seized by a feeling of absolute certainty about Joseph. It's hard to explain what I mean by "certainty." It's not a particularly explicable genre of feeling, though it seems that most of the artistic output of the world has been devoted to trying to explain it. I had developed passionate crushes before then, and have since, but to date this is the only time I have ever just known, in the same matter-of-fact way that you know any fact about yourself, that I was going to be with someone for a long time.

Or was it a self-fulfilling prophecy, did I force the issue? Possibly. There were plenty of opportunities, plenty of perfectly reasonable reasons, for us to split up during those first few years together. We ignored them. Partly because it was almost unimaginably scary to be navigating what we were navigating—being nineteen, twenty, twenty-one in a giant place that manifestly did not care whether we failed or succeeded—on our own, and partly because we were in love.

Actual memories of this time are hard to come by, too, and there are fewer snapshots. There's one of the giant American flag that the Hells Angels kept hung from the roof of their 3rd Street headquarters to the roof opposite all during that sad, heightened fall. Joseph is standing in the middle of the street under the flag, in profile, so you can see his Mohawk. His face looks puffy from too much late-night Chinese food and malt liquor, but even that and the haircut and the scruffy beard he'd grown over the summer can't conceal his youth and beauty. There is another picture, maybe from the same day, of him sitting on my "bed," which functioned during the day as a couch in the 3rd Street apartment. In this one he's wearing a stained white T-shirt and dark jeans that he was fastidious about not washing, so that they would attain a particular shape and retain a particular color. In this photo you can see the tattoo, an outlined band of stars, around his upper arm. I don't have the photo in front of me right now, and it's been a year since I last saw Joseph and I can't remember which arm the tattoo is on. But I can remember the exact pencil-shavings smell of his body and I feel as though I would recognize it anywhere.

In a way, it was Joseph's example that emboldened me to get start getting tattooed, because I loved the way all tattoos, but especially his tattoo, looked. We had only been sleeping together for a few weeks when I got my first one, a small broken heart over my right hipbone. I went to a place on Avenue A with my roommate Jenna, who wore raccoonlike rings of eyeliner and stacked moon boots at all times and generally cultivated an image of irreproachable hard-coreness. Halfway through getting an anchor that started right where her closely shaved hairline hit the back of her neck, she slumped to the floor in a faint. The tattoo artist calmly revived her with Coke and Skittles. When it was my turn I barely winced, and soon I had a permanent broken heart. It was emboldening in general to know that I could act nonchalant about pain. The next summer I did research and found the artist who has done all the work on my arms and shoulders, and she tattooed a pair of swimming Japanese carp on my back. I had been dividing my time between working at a "punk" bar where everyone had tattoos except me and sitting in that community garden on 6th Street, the one I'd seen from the director's apartment, staring at the fish in the koi pond. And then the next year I got a chrysanthemum on my shoulder and the poppies on that same arm, the ones strangers often mistake for heirloom tomatoes. But after that I didn't get anything more done until 2007. I couldn't decide what I wanted. I asked Joseph what he thought I should do next.

It was a strange conversation for us to be having; in a way it was strange that we were talking at all. A week earlier I had confessed to him that I'd kissed a coworker. After I'd confessed we had fought, and the fight was the pinnacle of a genre of fighting we had been practicing for years. It was as though we had been in training, meticulously ramping up intervals and capacities, and now finally we had made it, we were competing in the Olympics of eviscerating each other. All our fights now culminated at the same ecstatic pitch of hysteria that involves your entire body, all the potential of your body stretched to its utmost. We would scream at the top of our lungs and sob until we were too dehydrated to cry anymore, stubbornly maintaining whatever stupid positions we were defending for hours, until sheer exhaustion forced us into tenderness and reconciliation. This had, at one point, maybe years earlier, been sort of fun. Now it left me feeling scraped out, so that even the exhausted reconciliation part was hollow and the tenderness was rote and feigned.

I remember him kneeling, clutching his stomach, sobbing, asking why I'd even told him. I was sobbing too and saying, "I told you because I want to be with you! If I had wanted to leave you I wouldn't have told you!" which seems, in retrospect, obviously untrue. In the moment, though, I had meant it, or had thought I had.

In the aftermath of this fight we maintained the feigned, tentative tenderness for a week, and it began almost to seem that if we could just keep pretending things were fine, they might be fine. I was still sneaking off to make out with my coworker in alleys during the workday, but at night I put that out of my mind and focused on the time I was spending with Joseph. He was docile. He went with me to get his gnarly toenails professionally pedicured, which I had been nagging him to do for years, and the pedicure lady fawned over us and told us what a cute couple we were. We were exaggeratedly nice to each other. We didn't talk about anything. And at the end of that strange week we went to spend that long weekend in Nantucket with Joseph's entire extended family.

The house in Nantucket was outlandishly beautiful: gray-shingled, rose-trellised, with a roomful of antique cookbooks and turquoise-painted kitchen floors. It was another summery place where we'd been happy together in the past. And we tried, that weekend, to recapture the feeling we'd had there before—we faked it so well that, a couple of times, we made it. But when we talked about our future I couldn't stop myself from crying tears I tried to pretend were from relief, or joy. And on the last night when his family got into a fight at the boozy dinner table, Joseph, particularly drunk, failed to side with me on some idiotic issue or other. Back in our room I sulked and stared at the ceiling, and when he realized how upset I was he dissolved into drunken sobbing. He told me how difficult it was to be around his grandfather, who had never believed in him. I told him that I didn't care and that it was hard for me to be around his WASP family and I needed him in my corner. His nose was running. I wasn't crying at all this time.

The ache in my chest had calcified and become a numbness. Eventually Joseph cried himself to sleep; awake, I looked at him. I stared at the face I had looked at every day for years, the downy shaved scalp, the tender earlobes and strong, ropy neck. I couldn't imagine what it would be like when these things would not belong to me as intimately as parts of my own body. But these things couldn't belong to me unless so much else did, too, much of which I didn't want. "I am tired of having your problems be my problems," I thought. "I have enough problems of my own."

In the morning he didn't remember what he'd said, or that we'd fought at all.

I looked in the mirror as we were getting dressed and idly said something about how I was ready to get another tattoo, that I knew what it would be, two kinds of starfish, but that I didn't know where I wanted it to go. "Put it on the other arm and shoulder, balance it out. Symmetry," Joseph said. I wondered why I hadn't thought of such a simple solution before.

I made an appointment as soon as we got back into town, and two months later I went and had the work done, by which time I was living in my own apartment. It was odd not to have to worry, while changing my bandages that night, about someone else rolling over in bed and disturbing the thin temporary skin that protects the tattoo as it's healing. And it was long-sleeve weather by then, too, so it was months before anyone besides me even saw the new tattoos.

Sometimes you get a new haircut when you break up with someone. This wasn't like that. This was more like, I had been working on building myself a different skin the entire time we were together, with Joseph's help, but now I had become something entirely new. The whole time we were together, it turned out, I had been working on making myself into someone he wouldn't recognize.

The last time I saw Joseph was six months after our breakup, when we had dinner so that I could show him a draft of a story I was working on. The story mentioned our relationship and our breakup and I wanted to make sure there was nothing in it that he would object to, since it was being published in a venue where lots of people who'd know him would see it. Also, I wanted to have sex with him to see if we were still in love, but the conscious part of my brain was completely unaware of this. I had been at a fancy party earlier in the evening and I'd worn a borrowed strapless dress. Joseph was gaunt and pale, and the apartment we had shared was completely overtaken with his music equipment and records and ashtrays. He'd started smoking cigarettes again and was doing it compulsively, as most recidivist ex-smokers tend to do.

Before we sat down to look over the article we decided to have dinner at a restaurant down the block. We ordered a bottle of wine and Joseph made it clear that he would pay this time. Over dinner we talked about how easy it was to be in each other's company, how we'd spent long enough not having any contact with each other and that now we could interact like friends and how great was that? After we finished the wine we went back to the apartment, and it was strange to have to be *let in* to someplace I'd lived for four years. We sat down on the futon that he had moved into his room, which had been his studio when we'd lived together—a roommate lived in the room that had been our bedroom—and we shared a cigarette and I pretended to read something else while he looked over the printed-out pages of my article.

In the end there was nothing he objected to except he didn't want me to say how much pot we'd smoked, which I had no problem taking out. Then he played me some of the music he'd been working on since I'd left, which was better than anything he'd done while we were together. I think I must have stood up to go, and then he was like "Can I get a hug?" So we hugged.

The real damage wasn't done during that night we spent together on the crumb-covered futon, though. The mistake was that for the entire following day I stayed in the apartment, drinking tea out of our old mugs, working there on one of his computers. We ordered take-out and I borrowed clothes of his to wear home since I couldn't wear the strapless dress. In the middle of the day we had sex again, even though I had my period and a hangover and my hair was greasy and my eyes stung from keeping my contact lenses in for two days straight. When I finally forced myself to leave, he walked me to the subway, taking the scenic route around the block and walking up tree-lined India Street. I was squinting in the sunlight without sunglasses, feeling strange in his jeans and T-shirt and walking awkwardly with a wad of folded toilet paper stuffed in the crotch of my underpants. "We'll see each other again soon?" "Yes," I said. We said something about not wanting to lose each other again. We embraced and I turned back to watch him standing there smiling as I walked down the subway stairs.

A few days later Joseph called while I was in North Carolina visiting my younger brother at college. He wanted me to delete any mention of him from the story, he said. His mother, a recent law school graduate who'd never been one of my biggest fans, seemed to have prepared a lecture for him to give me—the words sounded like her quasi-legalistic jargon, not like anything he would say. I realized that I'd been wrong to show him the article in the first place, wrong to go see him, wrong to trust him, wrong to allow him to trust me. What he was saying now was crazy, and he sounded like a crazy person saying it. I haven't spoken to or heard from him since.

Sometimes when we were together we would make dinner and eat it in front of the TV and smoke a joint and then lapse into a happy daze of satiety and fall asleep leaning into each others' warm bodies. Sometimes we would stay up late just lying in bed and talking about whatever, like kids at a slumber party. Other times, Joseph would come home late from a show or a practice so trashed that I didn't want to be in the same room with his clammy, booze-sweating body, and then in the morning he would be sick, waking me every time he ran to the bathroom to retch, and I would feel so martyred and so helpful because I would go to the deli and get him a liter of ginger ale before leaving for work.

And then sometimes we would be at the beach, wrapped around each other in the saltwater, kissing and laughing into each others' mouths, feeling the same feelings at the same time.

It's not like our relationship was constructed solely

of any one of these experiences. If it had been, it might be easier to understand how someone whose body and needs and phone number I used to know better than my own is now a stranger to me, but I guess that's just how these things work.

In the car on the way back from our weekend at the beach, my mom was doing her usual thing of keeping up a steady stream of conversation at all times. A few years ago, during a misguided phase of thinking that honesty and not keeping things bottled up were the solutions to interpersonal problems, I told my mom that her tendency to externalize her internal monologue bothered me. I might as well have asked her to change her eye color or her handwriting.

On the way out of town, before we got out onto the long, flat country roads leading away from the coast, she talked about various health concerns and what I should do about retirement savings and foods you can eat to ensure that you get enough calcium and members of our family and different problems they'd been having, cycling through every possible topic on the off chance that, over the course of the weekend, we'd forgotten to discuss anything. But then, as we drove over the Chesapeake Bay

Bridge, without my even noticing it right away, we finally lapsed into a companionable silence.

Which I broke, for some reason. I looked out the window at the water, which on the narrow suspension bridge seems to swell toward your car, surrounding you on all sides, and I said, "It's so pretty."

"Isn't it? I love being near the water."

"I do too."

And then she asked, as if it was the inevitable, logical place the conversation ought to go next: "So, is Joseph still living with his parents?"

I told her the truth, which is that I don't know. I looked out into the water; we were almost at the mid-point of the bridge.

It's strange not to know where he lives. I have a couple of friends still who are friends with him but lately I don't even ask about his whereabouts or well-being when we hang out. For a while, I heard, he'd quit drinking and doing drugs entirely and was making music. I hope that wherever he is and whatever else he's doing he is still making music.

Once as a gift he recorded a My Bloody Valentine–sounding cover of the Fleetwood Mac song "Sentimental Lady" for me, his beautiful voice tentative and plangent under layers of distortion. A few days after I got back from North Carolina, after that final phone call, I was listening to my iTunes on random and the song came up, and I deleted it. The song was beautiful and now no one will hear it again. The past is not a place that you can visit. The present is destroying the past as every moment replaces the moment prior. But if I close my eyes and listen hard I can still hear Joseph's voice singing that song.

10

Claudine

On a warm night in May I went out to do karaoke at a tiny bar downtown. Because it was a weeknight I left early, just past midnight. It was too early and too nice out to justify taking a cab. A limo sprouting bachelorettes from its roof passed me, trailing squeals that echoed in the trafficless late-night street, and when they paused at a stoplight I laughed to hear the squeals abruptly dwindle. The city seemed half-deserted but in a cozy, shrunken way: unimpeachably safe. I decided I would walk to the L and take it to Williamsburg, where my bike was parked. I walked up Grand and turned right at Bowery.

I walked past boarded-up storefronts and glass-fronted new high-rises with chic restaurants in their ground levels. Below Houston there were snoozing homeless men and women lying under piles of filthy blankets under the scaffolding; across the street from them there were clean-cut, spray-tanned young people smoking cigarettes outside a club's velvet rope. One homeless man sat up under his blankets as I walked by and started shouting incoherently; I pushed my earbuds in deeper and turned up the volume on my iPod. It was playing Lou Reed, singing about cheap, cheap downtown dirt.

Peering in a glass-fronted restaurant's window, I thought about how the people inside the restaurant probably had totally different maps of the city in their heads than I do, and then I started thinking about how different—not inaccurate, exactly—my own mental map of the city had been when I first moved here, on a warm May day almost exactly eight years earlier.

That was the summer I lived on 3rd Street between First and Second Avenues. My first commute had been to a restaurant on the corner of Bleecker and Lafayette, which I somehow did not realize was a five minute walk away from my apartment, so I took the F train one stop to get there, from Second Avenue to Broadway Lafayette, emerging from the train right outside the restaurant's front door. I had lived in New York for about a week and a half and it was my first day of work as a hostess. I walked up out of the subway and saw, standing on that corner, the one person I knew in New York besides my roommates: the guy I'd had an overdramatic unrequited crush on at Kenyon, the one who would eventually inspire me to tattoo a broken heart on my hipbone. He was just standing there. Who knows what he was up to? Just living in New York, I guess. When he saw me the look in his eyes was very clearly like "Oh shit." I gave him a wincing smile and said "Hi?" and then hurriedly walked through the door and into the restaurant, where I spent the day failing to absorb anything the girl who was training me said.

So that corner ended up belonging to him, on my mental map. It's not an exaggeration to say that I spent the next few years expecting to run into that guy around that and every corner, but it never happened until years after I stopped looking, when I passed him on the street in Park Slope, looking sunburned and fat.

In the weeks that followed I built my map up piecemeal. Landmarks got flagged: places to get slices of pizza, bars that didn't card. I was transferred from the restaurant on Bleecker to a sister business, a steak house near Herald Square, and my map grew accordingly. I went to the H&M near the steak house to buy more all-black work outfits. I sat in the little park in the middle of Broadway across the street from Macy's and ate stolen rolls and smoked cigarettes. I was unhappy in my uneventful hostessing job; they paid me well and fed me and all I had to do was stand there for hours, smiling at the businessmen who came in for long, highly calorific lunches. So I quit after a few months to work as a shot girl at a dive on Third Avenue.

This job, at least, I could obviously walk to from my apartment. This became less of a consolation when, a few weeks in, I started having these visceral freak-outs during the walk over—I'd get nauseous and my heart would start pounding uncontrollably. It felt like stage fright; it was a sort of stage fright, I guess, because it usually went away as soon as I got to the bar and started performing. I walked around with my tray of test-tube shots, trying to provoke the crowd into sucking down hits of neon-colored liquid. "Only if you do one with us," was a common enough response to my shot-pushing come-on that I would secretly reserve an area of the tray for my special shots, which were watered-down enough that I could do twenty of them over the course of my shift. I still got drunk every night I worked there. Some girls would probably have been able to handle the constant onslaught of drunken misbehavior better than I did. I was trying to prove something to myself about how I was able to handle it, I guess. There was a bouncer whom I could summon to eject the guys who tried to touch me, but most of the time it didn't seem worth bothering him. I hardly ever think about this now, but when I do I think it's bizarre that I worked there. I think I did it because I felt like, as long as I look a way that attracts this kind of attention I might as well make some money off it. I didn't even make that much money.

What money I did make, though, I stuffed into a boxy green purse and brought home, where even at 4 A.M. Claudine lay on her futon on the floor reading something serious in the center of a ring of dirty coffee cups and ashtrays around her bed. I leaned over her and shook out the contents of the green purse, showering her with sticky dollar bills and saying, "We're rich! We're rich!"

Claudine and I had met at Shakespeare day camp the summer after fourth grade but we didn't become close until the summer before seventh grade, when we met again in musical theater day camp. Obviously we had in common that we were weirdos. At eleven I was much hammier than Claudine, more of a grinning, pageanty wanna-be child-star. Claudine had very little interest in gunning for the leading parts in the camp's recitals; her voice was ragged and her acting style was, in retrospect, avant-garde—Brechtian or something; anyway, it wasn't what the camp counselors were looking for. She had an uncontrollable halo of gold ringlets, the kind you can pull down and then release while making a "sproing!" sound, and a wardrobe of cutoffs and Converse and inherited tie-dye at a time when most people I knew wore matched outfits from the juniors' department of Sears or oversize

Looney Tunes T-shirts. Her house was a wood smoke–smelling Hobbit mansion filled with gorgeous old furniture and piles upon piles of books. We spent time in her mom's art studio and occasionally caught glimpses of her dad, an enormously tall man with a beard that met his mass of head-hair in a wide, frizzy lion's mane. The first time I spent the night there, I stayed up til dawn reading Steven King's *Carrie* and then was too deliciously frightened to sleep, so I just lay there smelling the old house and listening to it creak and settle.

The wall of Claudine's attic bedroom was covered with an ornate mural featuring strange fairies engaged in various strange activities, painted in her idiosyncratic, wobbly style. At the time I thought that I was a better drawer than Claudine in much the same way I thought I was a better actress: I could make smooth lines and realistic-looking faces, I could say my lines the same way the character did in the movie. I was not and am still not better than Claudine at anything.

In seventh grade we went to the same school for the first time. We were partners whenever a project called for partners; we "went out" with a pair of best friends, and we cowrote a romance novel titled *Moonlight on Three Mile Island* in a speckled composition book that we passed back and forth in school all day. We balled up tinfoil into the shape of an alien head and invented a religion devoted to worshipping this god, who we called

"Merv." We saluted each other by wiggling our fingers underneath our faces in a way that was meant to imitate a squid: "All hail (wiggle wiggle) Claudine (wiggle wiggle) demi-goddess of the underworld." Every few days Claudine would introduce me to some new strange thing that would change my life—she lent me books and made me mix tapes, she even recorded new songs off the radio and played them back to me over the phone. I remember hearing Nirvana for the first time this way. The best thing about our two-person subculture was that while obviously we were not cool by anyone else's standard, we seemed enormously cool to each other. When this period eventually ended it was because Claudine had become cool in the outer world, too.

The first step towards Claudine's becoming cool was that she became bad. A duller light suffused the Hobbit house now, making what had been cozy clutter seem chaotic and awry. Soon Claudine's perfect pale calves were crisscrossed with thin, white razor lines that were meticulous in a way that her schoolwork was not. She picked physical fights and threw herself on the ground in an ecstasy of fake convulsions. She started hanging out with Janna Karapowski, the prettiest girl in our grade, one of those preternaturally voluptuous middle-schoolers whose bodies basically give them no option but to go out with high school boys and smoke cigarettes, and also with a pack of girls who were drama geeks in a different way than we were, whose drama geekness involved lace gloves and clove cigarettes and ornate eyeliner.

I was still a little bit too much of a kid, or, I was trying too hard, or my family life was too stable and normal—a little of everything, I guess. By the end of eighth grade we had become so distant that at one point Claudine handed me an invitation to a party Janna Karapowski was throwing, the kind of party where you sensed that parental presence would be minimal, and while handing it to me said, "But, you know, it would probably be better if you didn't come."

Then ninth grade came and I went to the magnet public high school, which, thanks to her grades, was not an option for Claudine, who went to Quaker private school. At the Quaker school she was not forced to take math or wear shoes. She became friends with troubled people, and watched as small and incredibly large tragedies befell them. Nothing very bad happened to Claudine, but the consequences her friends suffered made her kinder, or seemed to. Claudine came back into my life toward the end of high school, just pulled up in my parents' driveway one day in one of her father's junkyard cars, which looked cool but reeked of motor oil so badly that you had to drive around with all the windows open, even in winter. I hadn't realized how much I had missed her. My other friends' idea of fun was renting romantic comedies and watching them while gorging on treats from the bulk bins of Safeway; Claudine would take me to some party where there were twenty year olds and beer. My parents, understandably, hated her.

So they were unthrilled to learn, a few years later, that I planned to move in with Claudine, in New York. Through my years of school in Ohio we had maintained a correspondence, e-mailing and even sometimes calling each other on the phone. Before every school break people who were driving to points East would send out all-student e-mails offering up the free seats in their cars in exchange for gas money, and so I would get rides to stay with Phillip at Sarah Lawrence or with Claudine in the East Village, in the cramped two-bedroom she shared with two other girls, one of whom lived in the living room. This was the roommate I replaced when Claudine called to ask if I wanted to move in.

That summer was unbearably hot and we had only fans to cool our tiny, airless apartment. Once I came home late at night and, peering past the open door of Claudine's bedroom, was scandalized to see sleeping Claudine sprawled naked on her mattress on the floor, a pile of pale curves that stunned me with their pink vulnerability. I considered myself lucky not to have caught a similar glimpse of her boyfriend.

Arnie habitually wore a porkpie hat and he had a goatee and disproportionately thick calves from his off-and-on pedicabbing gig. By biking cartloads of tourists through midtown he earned enough money to keep himself in plastic-wrapped honey bun pastries (the only thing I ever saw him consume besides coffee) and pouches of rolling tobacco and baggies of cheap, seedy pot. It was not, of course, enough money to pay rent anywhere. Though many of his friends were college students, he himself was not one. He was twenty-four, which seemed old to us but not, I guess, to the older women whose hospitality he had enjoyed before Claudine became his girlfriend. He was also friends with a coterie of old-school East Village eccentrics, publishers of alternative magazines, and operators of art theaters who clung to the relics of the neighborhood they'd known even as its rents became stratospheric and its dive bars and zine shops became fancy restaurants and baby boutiques. He was working on a novel, and Claudine spent a lot of her time helping him to edit it, crouching over the typewritten pages with an expression of intense focus. I read some of the pages, too, fresh from the typewriter that Arnie kept in Claudine's room. It was innovative the way he played with syntax and grammar, I guess. His work was poststructural, postpunctuational. I felt bad for not understanding the appeal of what I knew must be great work. I didn't think that Claudine, the smartest person I knew, would be wasting her time on crap. At night I lay in bed and tried not to hear the noises coming from her room for what seemed like hours on end.

Arnie's ministrations made Claudine swollen and dowdy. She wore her glasses more and stayed inside, chain-smoking. Our apartment was colonized by Arnie's books and the furniture he dragged in off the sidewalk; the butts of his cigarettes stayed where he extinguished them on the lip of the bathtub. Eventually, I moved out, but not without telling Claudine exactly what I thought she was doing wrong. Just like in eighth grade, we took a hiatus from our friendship, reuniting later on terms that, though never formally negotiated, were subtly different than they had been before I alienated her.

The other night I rode my bike to Greenpoint to meet Claudine for dinner. We don't have mutual friends anymore and we rarely have much in common with each others' friends and boyfriends, so we meet for these dinners every once in a while, saying each time at the end that we won't let so much time pass before the next one. Sometimes these dinners are full of easy intimacy and intense teenagerish simpatico-ness, and sometimes they are as awkward as first dates, for reasons I've never quite been able to figure out.

This was the first time I'd been to the northernmost tip of Brooklyn in a while and the first time I'd ever gotten there via bike. I've only been riding a bike since I moved to Clinton Hill. Greenpoint is one of the most eminently bikeable neighborhoods in New York, with its wide, bike-laned avenues and plethora of barely trafficked side streets. If I'd had a bike during the four years I'd lived there, my cumulative saved commuting time would probably add up to something spectacular: a month of my life, maybe two, unwasted. All the time I spent craning my neck and peering down Manhattan Avenue, hoping for a glimpse of the B61—and then all the time I spent crammed onto the trundling bus, smelling strangers and being irritated by their cell phone conversations—could have been spent in healthy motion, with every part of my brain and body engaged in the project of getting to my destination. Why did no one tell me this? Why didn't I figure it out on my own? This is one of the most painful things about getting older, especially getting older in the same place where you were young: the constant realizations that you could have been doing everything better all along, if only you'd known how to read the map more accurately.

I had some version of all these thoughts as I rode to the end of the island. The sun was low in the sky and the views of Manhattan and Long Island City were somehow more spectacular from the middle of the street than they'd ever been from the sidewalk.

From a distance I watched Claudine walk towards me

as I clumsily locked my bike to the lamp post in front of the restaurant. She was looking quintessentially Claudiney in a skimpy old dress that revealed the tattoo of seaweed from Ernst Haeckel's Art Forms in Nature on her upper chest. Her hair was haloed out around her face by the summer humidity even though the temperature was dropping. We went inside the restaurant, a Mexican dive, and sat down at a sticky table.

She asked how I'd been and I said everything had been really boring, then proceeded to talk about myself for the next twenty minutes. When I finally stopped talking she quietly told me that she was getting married.

Instead of feeling happy for her I wondered immediately why she hadn't told me sooner, then answered my own question by asking her lots of second-guessy questions.

After dinner we walked across the Pulaski Bridge from Brooklyn to Queens, to see a show in Long Island City. We climbed the red metal staircase that leads to the walkway and were walking high above the muddy waterway below, with the traffic almost drowning us out and bikes coming up behind us every few minutes, shouting "On your left!" It finally occurred to me about halfway across the bridge to congratulate her.

Later, after the show, after we walked back across the bridge, when Claudine and I were saying good-bye outside the restaurant where I'd parked my bike, she said something about how in previous eras we would both have married the people we'd spent our early twenties living with, and how it was good that we hadn't. I agreed with her but thought to myself that I didn't know that it would have made much difference, ultimately, except that we would have had to pay for lawyers and divorces. I walked my bike with her for a few blocks, then turned off and rode down Freeman Street. She had done everything before I had, and I had followed her, using her example to gauge what might be possible. But I had made a mistake, probably, when I thought that one of us could mark a path for the other to follow.

Claudine wrote a play a few years ago that I remember well because I saw it three times, once at a dress rehearsal and twice during its official run, not out of a sense of friendly obligation but because I loved being in the world of the play and was trying to cement it in my mind. She performed in the play alongside another small-boned girl with childlike features clustered in the center of her face. This girl and Claudine played persecuted children, sisters on the run from some kind of tall, hairy monster. The dialogue was twisty and difficult, stylized and rhythmical, but not so far outside the realm of normal speech that the virtuosity called attention to itself. The sets and the costumes and even the expressions on the characters' faces looked like the paintings on Claudine's childhood bedroom wall. Claudine had had an imaginary world inside her as long as I'd known her and now here it was, made visible for an audience, who peered in, entranced.

On the last night I came to see the play I stood afterwards with the smokers on the sidewalk, waiting until Claudine came out, still in her stage makeup, looking outlandishly beautiful. For a moment I hesitated to approach her, the way one hesitates to approach an admired celebrity. It's hard, sometimes, to love a person who you have to share with the world. They're yours, for a moment, in a café or at your kitchen table, and then they're on a stage and you are the same to them as anyone else in the theater, even if you've made a point of coming early and sitting in the front row.

11

The Lens

I had been fine for a year, more than a year, and then at Vicki's wedding reception a dark familiar thing stood near me, breathing hard, and I was standing half in the sun and half in its shadow, not sure whether I'd be able to fight it off. Maybe this thought only occurred to me because the wedding reception was being held in an occult bookstore, but it reminded me of the sick, hopeless, bone-chilled feeling Harry Potter gets around "dementors," which are these black-hole wraiths that suck happiness out of the world and can only be defeated by a spell that entails thinking powerful positive thoughts.

That sounds so lame; it makes more sense in the world of those books, where powerful positive thoughts can assume the shape of a giant silver stag. In the real world, dementors can't be vanquished by conjuring one's most vivid happy memories. Deep breaths, trips outside to get some air, little chalky buttons of Ativan that I pulverize between my molars in case that will make them work faster: these do something, certainly, but they don't exactly fix or end the feeling. My former therapist Susan only ever promised that anti-anxiety medication would "take the edge off," which is a good way of putting it. I really liked Susan, but I would be thrilled never to see her again. I suspect I'll see her again, though: that's just the nature of these things. I'm not supposed to wait so long the next time, she told me after the last time: "Come to me before you're lying on the kitchen floor." The lying on the kitchen floor is a bit of a joke now, ever since I wrote an article about having panic attacks in a variety of unsanitary locations: my boyfriend teases me about it sometimes. We've been together for a while now and I've never had a panic attack in front of him; I wonder what it will be like when I do.

What was it about the wedding reception that slipped that icicle down the back of my dress? It's true that, like a lot of people, I get a bit freaked out by weddings. This one had been remarkably low-key, though, as these things go: a ten-minute ceremony in a public park, to be followed by pizza and beer and a homemade cake shaped like Alf saying "Congratulations from Melmac," served in the occult bookstore.

That morning the bride and groom had led a group of their friends and relatives though the park to a clearing near an old elm tree, and then there we were: outside at midday on the first uncomfortably warm day of summer, me and a bunch of strangers in party clothes and makeup that was going to look a lot better when we weren't standing in direct sunlight. A disproportionate number of the women, myself included, were wearing the kind of high-waisted dresses that some intrepid vintage-clothing shopkeeper finds in a thrift store and marks up. The park's smells of grass and concrete wafted toward me on a breeze, combined with the hot human smells of perfume and cigarette smoke and sweat being absorbed by polyester. Everyone was swatting away gnats, and when Vicki almost stepped on a dead rat that was lying at the base of the elm everyone giggled. For a minute the whole thing seemed like a joke, a joke about getting married. Even as the ceremony started it kept seeming like a joke because Carl, the groom, kept his sunglasses on the whole time and cocked his head like he was coolly reluctant to be there, answering the officiant's rote questions with a clipped "Sure." There were a couple of readings, one funny and one heartfelt, and the heartfelt one seemed out of place.

Then the officiant, a burly guy with a nickname,

handed Carl a little ring. It had diamonds in the band, and they sparkled in a beam of sunlight that sluiced photogenically through the canopy of the tree with the dead rat at its base. And you could see Carl's hand shake as he took Vicki's hand. Vicki is a tall, thin girl but she has these tiny, fat-fingered white hands like you see in stylized portraits from a certain era. Carl took her white, girlish hand and pushed the ring up and onto the base of her finger, nestling it into the soft flesh there. Then they looked at each other, or at least, it seemed that they did—he was still wearing his sunglasses—and he squeezed her ringed hand, and tears sprang to my eyes as automatically as they do when an aesthetician rips off the first strip of wax below the arch of my eyebrow. As Vicki slipped Carl's ring onto his hand, I wiped my eyes and darted my gaze to either side to see whether I was alone in crying. I regained my composure easily, in the same embarrassed way I do at the waxing place.

For several years, when my mom was just beginning to work as a lawyer, my brother and I spent time after school at the homes of various day-care ladies. Some of them were wonderful—I especially liked the ones who had their own kids, especially if they were girls and older than me—but one of them never fed us any snacks except teddy bear–shaped graham crackers, and the other kids she took care of were toughs who mocked me because I didn't know the word *fuck*. I was in kindergarten.

The main activity at her house was watching the TV that was always on and tuned to daytime soaps. In this way I developed an early understanding of sex that contained a lot of misperceptions, chief among them one that I didn't find out the truth about until much later, when a girl with whom I was playing house explained to me that pregnancy was not directly caused by a magic spell that the priest uttered during the wedding ceremony. Even after she explained what *did* cause pregnancy, I persisted in thinking of the wedding ceremony as some kind of spell until years later, or maybe I never stopped.

The night before the wedding all the guests sat in Vicki's backyard, the girls drinking PBR through penis straws in a token nod to bachelorette party–ness. Vicki's friend Alice sat down next to me. She was a pretty girl with a round, childish face, the kind with no bad angles, and a pixie haircut. Via the penis straws we got into a conversation about penis size, which segued into a conversation about dating. We were not on our first PBRs at this point. Alice told me about a relationship she'd had with a bike messenger that had been based mainly on e-mails and sex, which had both been of above-average quality. But the relationship, such as it was, had ended, mainly because of the dude's terrible body odor. Still, she said, she was happy that she had been able to enjoy this person's company without developing feelings for him. When she ran into him now, they were genuinely happy to see each other. But she hoped, in the future, not to have any more completely meaningless sex, though she was also hoping to hook up with the groom's brother that night. (Reader, she fellated him.)

Through this recounting I was feeling a bit restless—I was tired and ready to leave the party, except I was sleeping at Vicki's that night, so leaving the party was impossible. So to keep things interesting I asked Alice whether she thought she would ever get married.

"I really don't know," she said. "I sort of don't think so."

"Yeah, I sort of don't think I will either," I said, and it was the first time I'd ever said this aloud, or even realized that I thought it. But, you know, I do. How can anyone stand there and say "forever," knowing that it's possible to feel the way Vickie and Carl feel and then, eventually, not to?

I was at a party in the backyard of a bar in Williamsburg a few days before I broke up with Joseph, having a great time until I happened to blink in such a way that my contact lens folded in half and got stuck to the inside of my eyelid. This had never happened to me before, so it took me a minute to figure out what was going on. I went to

the bathroom and tried, in the dim red light there, to figure out how to pull the lid away from the eyeball enough
so that the itchy shard of plastic could slip back out from
underneath it. Through the little barred window in the
bathroom I could hear the party noises from the backyard. Frantic, I scratched my eyeball with a ragged fingernail and winced. I realized I was going to have to go
home and deal with the situation.

By the time I walked through the front door of the
Greenpoint apartment my eye was red and continuously
oozing tears, and the unpleasant tickle under the lid had
turned to a dry, stabbing pain. Joseph was sitting on the
couch with a packet of rolling tobacco and a baggie of
pot in front of him, rolling a joint. Since the revelation of
spending three days without smoking pot in Fire Island
and not missing it, I had been trying to see how long I
could extend my sobriety, but it was hard with Joseph
around to tempt me. He waved the finished joint in my
direction, but I told him that neither of us could smoke
it because what if I had to go to the emergency room to
remove the contact lens from where it had lodged behind
my optic nerve, in my brain? I went into the bathroom
and tried to pry it out again, gave up, and started to cry
from both eyes. In the other room, Joseph had opened
up his laptop and was Googling instructions for how to
remove a stuck contact lens. "Just relax," he said, and I
ratcheted up the intensity of my sobs. "It says you just

have to relax and let it drift back down into place. It can't actually go behind your eyeball, you know. I'll go get some saline solution. Is there anything else you want from the deli?"

"Maybe some ice cream," I said, sniffling. When the door clicked closed behind him I started crying harder again, because of how nice was he being and how I didn't deserve him. He came back with the saline solution, which dislodged the lens in seconds. Tearstained and wearing glasses, I curled up on the sofa and stretched my legs across his lap in one of the many companionable poses we rotely assumed that used parts of the other person's body as furniture. We smoked the joint and ate the ice cream and fell asleep in front of the TV.

In the last year of our relationship, after I started working at Gawker, things got less and less fine so quickly. I'd gone back to seeing Susan once a week after I started having panic attacks again, and often during lulls in my one-sided conversation with her I thought of mentioning that I smoked pot every day. It just kept seeming like not the best possible moment to bring it up, though. Also, I had been cautioned against telling her by a friend who also liked to smoke pot on a regular basis: "If you tell your therapist, she'll just try to make everything be about that," the friend had said. I did wonder whether Susan might be in a position to confirm my suspicion that the moments each day when I felt unpleasantly attacked by even benign stimuli might be related to the hours of each day I spent substantially numbed to all experience, but wary of making "everything be about that," I kept not bringing it up.

There were still good times; there were good times all the time. For every night when we'd have some addled, slow-motion fight about how Joseph's job was going nowhere or how he spent most of his nights endlessly "practicing" but mostly just drinking with his improvisational noise-rock band that never played shows, there would be a day we spent lying on the couch in his studio, baked, listening to *The Dreaming* on his perfect stereo system and hearing all its subtlest textures and noticing its deepest themes for the first time. Where else would I ever find a boy who would love Kate Bush and Fleetwood Mac?, I would think whenever we had one of our recurring fights about housework or money or how fundamentally unethical my job was. He was wrong about the housework and the money, but he was right about my job, of course. Unfortunately, I was not ready to hear that just then. It was much more comfortable to talk about this with someone who completely understood both the downsides and the appeal of my job. Someone like: someone who had the same job, for example.

The morning after I got my contact stuck under my eyelid, I woke up next to Joseph's tall, lanky body in bed next to mine. As usual I had to wake up early and he was allowed to sleep in; I would always lie in bed for a few extra moments, watching him sleep. I got up and got dressed and ready for work, then came back around to the side of the bed to kiss him awake; this was his alarm clock. I breathed in his warm, sleepy smell and touched the bristles of his close-shaved head, admiring the defenseless, private look of him without his glasses. And then I went to work and betrayed him, and broke up with him and still betrayed him, and I am betraying him again now, writing this.

No one was standing near the counter of the occult bookstore, because the pizza and beer were on the other side of the room. So I stood there, leaning against the counter, looking away from the crowd, slowly calming down. Some oversize art and photography books were displayed near the cash register. I picked one of them up: it was a thick catalogue of Nan Goldin's photographs of her dissolute young friends in the East Village and Berlin and Provincetown in the late '70s and '80s.

Goldin has written that these photographs are about the tragedy inherent in love and dependency: "I often fear that men and women are irrevocably strangers to each other . . . but there is an intense need for coupling in spite of it all." Some of the photographs are just disgusting, like the close-up of a shaved pudenda with a fresh incision right above it, titled *Ectopic Pregnancy Scar.* In other photographs, filthy sheets and sinks full of dishes and couples with their eyes closed in heroin- or love-addled bliss stand out starkly against livid red or green walls. Most of the photographs in the book were familiar to me from the *Ballad of Sexual Dependency* slide show that plays perpetually in a small dark room on the second floor of the Museum of Modern Art but some I had never seen before, or had only seen in tiny online versions.

The most affecting of these photos are of the actress and writer Cookie Mueller at her wedding, and after. Goldin took many other photos of Cookie: in one her insane blond hair is backlit by neon in a bar, and another catches her maniacal openmouthed laughter as she crouches, pissing in an alley. In these she looks like just another of Goldin's standard leonine, hard party girls—unusually charismatic and lovely but essentially unserious, drifting fun and careless through her adventurous life. In the wedding photos, though, her hair is still wild but her eyes are different. In one frame they're filled with tears as she stands beside her beaming new husband, Vittorio. She's wearing little white lace fingerless gloves and her fingernails are garishly painted and bitten to the quick. Three years later Vittorio was dead; had they known he had HIV when they married? It was still early in the history of AIDS then, and people didn't know as much about the disease as they do now.

In Goldin's last photo of Cookie she is standing over Vittorio's open casket, blurry in the flashless shot and almost unrecognizable, so gaunt that she looks like a sad skeleton. Goldin has written that by this point Cookie was too sick even to speak. But she looks into the coffin with the same expression she'd worn at the wedding: love and sadness, twined together so tightly they are indistinguishable.

Acknowledgments

Thank you Mom and Dad and Ben Gould and all the extended Gould and Deshler clan.

Thanks to everyone at Free Press especially Amber Qureshi, Ali Pisano, Jill Siegel, Dominick Anfuso, and Martha Levin. Thanks to Mel Flashman.

Thanks to my teachers Deborah Wolk and Allison West, and everyone at Y.U.

Thank you Keith Gessen and Ruth Curry, for reading and fixing.

Thank you Bennett Madison, Normandy Sherwood, Alice Wetterlund, Lori Shprecher, Doree Shafrir and Leon Neyfakh.

Thank you Will Schwalbe and Choire Sicha, bosses extraordinaire.

Thanks to my friends. It pains me not to list you all, but I tried and then got too paranoid about leaving someone out and offending him or her. Sorry. I love you.

Thanks and apologies to H.B.T.

About the Author

EMILY GOULD is from Silver Spring, Maryland. Her writing has appeared in *The New York Times Magazine* and on her blog, Emilymagazine.com. She lives in Brooklyn.